mom

Grace

Holly Lomelino

mom Grace

experiencing the gifts of motherhood

Holly Lomelino

Sea Hill Press
Santa Barbara

*Dedicated to Krissy Mason, my oldest spiritual "daughter"
who has become one of my best friends. Watching you
become a mom has been such a joy and delight! Thanks
for being one of the greatest gifts God has given to me in
motherhood. You have been worth every bit of labor!*

Scripture quotations taken from the New American Standard Bible®,
Copyright © 1960, 1962, 1963, 1968, 1971, 1972, 1973, 1975, 1977, 1995
by The Lockman Foundation
Used by permission. (www.Lockman.org)

Sea Hill Press Inc.
P.O. Box 60301
Santa Barbara, California 93160
www.seahillpress.com

ISBN 978-1-937720-29-2

Printed in the United States of America

Contents

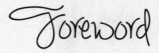

Foreword

It is such an honor that God has so graciously allowed me to write this book. I feel very disqualified to write it, because like many of us moms out there, I struggle daily with feeling like I am not yet the mom I want to be. I will be the first to admit that I do NOT have it all figured out. I make many mistakes every day. I don't do a good job always remembering the truths I am writing about. So this book is for me just as much as it for my readers. It has been a book to encourage me to live out the very perspective changes I know God has been graciously challenging me to learn.

Changing our perspective is not an easy thing to do. The awareness of truth is the first step, but to really begin to live out God's grace in motherhood means the truths have to become a part of us. I want to encourage you to take your time as you read through this book and really meditate on the perspective shifts offered in each chapter. I have included a journal page at the end of each one for writing down your own personal thoughts, prayers, and reflections on that particular gift. My encouragement is that you pause long enough to let God speak to you and personally minister to you about that gift in your own journey of motherhood. It is through this process that we will truly be changed.

Introduction

GRACE = GIFT

Grace is a word that is often misused. Grace is not our "get out of jail free" card. It is not some weak notion of God turning a blind eye to our wickedness. In fact, I don't believe it even has that much to do with our wickedness at all. Mercy is the concept of not getting what we deserve (the exemption from punishment that was what we had coming). Grace, however, is something entirely different. Grace is about getting a huge amount of what we *don't* deserve—and it's all good!

I think substituting the word *gift* for *grace* tends to help us get a better grip on what we are actually talking about. Grace involves all the multitude of gifts God has poured out upon us as His children.

Of course the greatest gift of all is salvation and the right to become children of God (John 1:12). Being adopted into His family and coming to know our Father, His Son, and the Holy Spirit is the best gift of grace there is. Yet the amazing thing about it is that He doesn't stop there. Romans 8:32 tells of this reality when Paul says, "He who did not spare His own Son, but delivered Him over for us all, how will He not also with Him freely give us all things?"

So many Christians seem to have a very limited perception of grace. They will believe in God's grace to save them from sin and death because of the work Jesus did on the cross for them (though many believers still think they have to earn God's approval by their actions). But few believe Him for the power to live out this life of faith, nor do they realize the inheritance they now have as children of God.

Being a mom is the hardest thing I have ever done. As a result, it has tested my perception of God's grace more than just about anything else in my life. But God has continually grown my understanding of just how big His grace is and how much He has given me and continues to give me as a mom.

When I cry out to God, "Give me grace!" throughout the day, I am not asking God to give me forgiveness. What I am asking for is His power and His supernatural ability to come in and make the impossible possible. Sometimes I use the terms "there was a grace for" something or "the grace was lifted." What I am referring to is God's supernatural gifts and empowering. Whether it is a grace for a certain friendship, or an activity I have the kids involved in, or a particular method of doing our chores, He is making it work! Or when the grace lifted, it meant that His empowering was gone (so I had better stop)!

I have written this book purely by His grace. I honestly can't even tell you how I was able to fit time to write a book into a crazy life with five kids, a busy ministry, homeschooling, a wedding coordinating business, and the myriad of other things that always seem to be going on. Yet, at the same time, I *can* tell you. It has been completely by His grace—a supernatural empowering and gift from Jesus.

Recently, I was talking with someone who mentioned accomplishing something by investing time into it, or if we don't have the time, investing money into it instead. I laughed and told her I had neither, but what I did have was the grace of God! As I said it, I knew that it was all I actually needed. When we rely on our own abilities, or our time or money, for example, we are not accessing what is needed to live a supernatural and impossible life. My kids and I love the verse where Jesus says, "With people this is impossible but with God all things are possible" (Matt. 19:26). There is something in us as believers that longs to access the supernatural ability to make the impossible possible. And that is the *grace of God!*

The purpose of this book is to take a look at some of the multitude of graces—or gifts—God has given us as moms. Some of the gifts are given up front, straight from His hand. Others are gifts that God gives us through the process of motherhood, as He walks us through its many challenges. These gifts are the ones that might never come to us if it weren't for the journey we are on.

It is easy as moms to notice the struggles. It is not hard to find something to complain about. And it often is a journey where we feel alone, experiencing very little encouragement or sympathy along the road. We wonder if we can ever get a break, and sometimes feel as though we may never make it. But my challenge to us—I definitely have to include myself—is to leave behind those ways of thinking. We must allow our perspective to shift from an earthly mindset to a heavenly one. We need to recognize the grace God is giving us and let Him transform the way we see our motherhood and everything it entails.

As you read, my prayer for you is that God would begin to open your eyes to the reality of His grace in your life. May we all come to recognize the vastness of His love and the abundance of His gifts, that we may more readily receive them and praise Him more exuberantly!

Chapter 1

THE GIFT OF FAITH

Stepping into motherhood takes great courage and faith. However, many of us probably became mothers without really realizing what we were getting ourselves into! I think that is all part of God's design to keep us from backing out because of fear. We want a cute little baby because of some strange God-given desire to nurture and care for another human being. But it is only after that precious child is inside of us that we start to experience the pain and sacrifice truly involved in motherhood.

For me it began right when the books say it should—at six weeks of pregnancy. That feeling of "all-day sickness" (mine never cooperated enough to only visit me in the mornings!) hit me strong. I soon discovered that everything I tried to eat tasted disgusting, and yet eating was the only thing that made me feel even a tiny bit better. It was like some cruel trick, having to eat all the time even though it's the last thing I wanted to do! Not to mention the fact that I normally love the taste of food and usually would be happy to have to be eating all the time! Then there are the aches and pains that come as your body changes in all sorts of ways and shapes. In addition to that, there is the way the growing belly makes walking, sitting, and even getting up a whole new challenge!

But it's really the birth that is the true introduction into motherhood, and rightly so. I've had five completely natural births and have enjoyed every one of them. I've also never experienced anything as intense as childbirth either. On top of that, I have begun to think that motherhood in general has been one long experience of labor in some ways!

When my first baby was finally delivered after a twenty-four-hour labor, I thought the hard work was done. But it wasn't until I tried to get a little sleep after the exhausting birth that I realized the real work was just beginning. As I was about to fall asleep, my newborn baby was brought back to me from the nursery and wanted to nurse, AND needed his diaper changed, AND needed to be comforted and swaddled, AND needed a lot of help to get back to sleep. And it wasn't but an hour later that he woke up and the whole cycle began again. So much for the dreamy-eyed vision of motherhood I had two days earlier when I was anxiously waiting for my baby to be born! *This* labor was never going to end!

In fact, it took a whole year of merciless sleep issues with my firstborn to finally get a respite from that original twenty-four-hour labor that first brought him into the world. Yet somehow I managed to keep trusting Jesus enough to be willing to get pregnant again, and it was just at that year mark that I did. So my journey of faith in motherhood continued, with a need for just that much more faith to trust God to provide what I needed to mother yet another gift from Him.

Today, almost ten years later, it still takes great courage and faith for me to even get out of bed in the mornings. Knowing that a full day with five needy children awaits me forces me to look to the only One who can truly give me what I need to be victorious today. Yet God in His goodness has given me a gift through motherhood—a strong and powerful faith. This faith has not come from taking the easy road, living a life of ease and comfort. Instead it has come from embracing the call to lay my life down for another, to sacrifice and trust that somehow through all the challenges and sleepless nights, it will all be worth it one day. It is a faith that takes God at His Word. He says that children are a blessing, a gift from His hand (Psalm 127), and He assures us that He will never leave us nor forsake us (Hebrews 13:5). He also promises to be our strength and our strong tower that we can run into when we are in need (Psalm 28:7 & Proverbs 18:10).

Having children and embracing the call to motherhood has stretched and challenged me in a way that few other things could. It has caused me to put my money where my mouth is and to trust Jesus in a whole new way. This has taken great faith and I know it will continue to take even greater faith.

I know that the faith and trust in Jesus that I need to deal with sleepless nights cannot even begin to compare with the faith I will need to deal with teenagers who want to start making their own way in the world. Yet no matter what challenges I will face as a mother, I must continue to rest in the One who gave me this job in the first place. I have had to learn how to surrender my children to the Lord and entrust them to Him instead of trying to do it all myself.

He has shown His faithfulness to me so many times as I have put my faith in Him throughout my journey. Whether it was having the faith to have another baby (despite what my feelings or circumstances said), or having the faith to believe Him for a van that would hold our growing family (of which I now have watched God do three times as three different people have given us vans in our journey), or having the faith to believe God for the energy and strength to be a mom of five children, He has proven Himself to be so faithful over and over again.

God,
Thank You for the opportunity to grow in my faith
by stretching me daily as a mom. Help me to continue to
trust You in each challenge that comes my way. Remind me
that You are enough and that Your strength is made perfect
in my weakness; that You will empower me to fulfill this
task and give me the grace I need to accomplish
what You have called me to.
Amen.

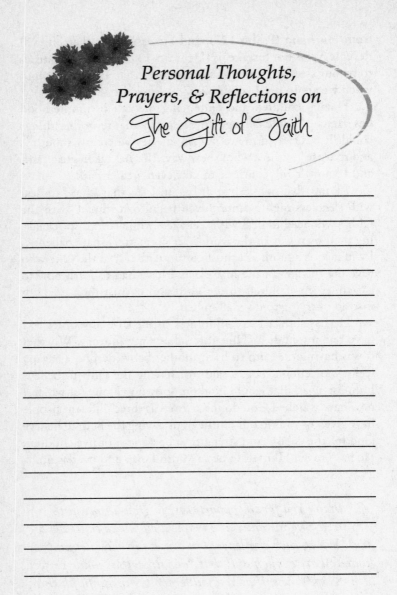

Personal Thoughts,
Prayers, & Reflections on
The Gift of Faith

_____

_____

_____

_____

_____

_____

_____

_____

_____

_____

_____

_____

_____

_____

_____

_____

"For we walk by faith, not by sight."

2 Corinthians 5:7

Chapter 2

THE GIFT OF HIS PRESENCE

One of my life verses comes out of Exodus, where Moses says to God before he sets out to go into the promised land, "If Your presence does not go with us, do not lead us up from here" (Ex. 33:15). In the preceding verse, God had already declared to Moses, "My presence shall go with you, and I will give you rest" (Ex. 33:14). Yet Moses was so adamant about needing God's presence that he wanted to confirm it and told God not to even send them if His presence did not go too.

In motherhood, God's presence is one of the greatest gifts we have. When I wake up in the morning, the cry of my heart should always be "God, give me Your presence!" I can't do it without Him, and I need Him with me every step of the way. Thankfully, in the New Covenant we have been given the Holy Spirit and therefore His presence is a gift we most assuredly have. I just need to be awakened to the reality of this gift in each moment.

When I try to handle life on my own, it doesn't take long to realize it is going to fail miserably. Do you ever have one of those days when everything just seems like it's going wrong? For me, it tends to be the days when I wake up and decide that I am going to set out to try to accomplish a whole bunch of stuff. I think it is God's way of showing me that if I try to do things in my own strength, it isn't going to work. I've found that the secret is resting in Him and letting Him be the One to do it *through me*.

Of course it doesn't mean everything goes perfectly on those days where I am resting in His presence; it just means that I will actually be able to breathe and have some semblance of joy and sanity throughout the day. I will be able to operate out of a place of peace and rest as I embrace His nearness.

While God's presence is actually synonymous with the Holy Spirit, I want to also briefly mention some of the specific gifts we have available in the Holy Spirit. These are not necessarily the list of spiritual gifts Paul makes mention of in 1 Corinthians 12, but they are gifts of who the Holy Spirit is to us. Among many things, He is our helper, counselor, and comforter.

Jesus told His disciples in John 14:16-17, "I will ask the Father, and He will give you another **Helper**, that He may be with you forever; that is the Spirit of truth . . . you know Him because He abides with you and will be in you." I don't know about you, but as a mother, a "constant helper" is exactly what I am in need of! There are so many days, in fact, so many moments in a day, where I am desperate for help. It has been such a relief to learn that I *have* a helper. Of course it would be great if my helper could also wash dishes and change diapers, but the fact that my Helper lives in me and can give me strength and courage to go on when I feel like I have nothing left to give is of much greater value than a physical helper who can do work for me. I have had times where I literally felt like I could not get up and finish cleaning the kitchen that desperately needed tending to. But as I have cried out to God to help me, I have experienced His help in such a supernatural way. Sometimes it has felt like He has almost carried me to the kitchen and given me supernatural strength to get things done.

He is also our **Counselor.** He can bring me wisdom and truth when I have no idea what to do, think, or say. Motherhood brings with it so many moments of decision-making, and I often am unsure of what to do. But knowing that I have access to the mind of God and can seek His wisdom and truth is such a gift. I do not want to take this for granted or neglect this incredible gift that God has given me. Recently one of my children got in a real funk and was struggling a lot with his attitude. He would get very angry over any little thing he was asked to do, and had become quite sassy and disrespectful. Thankfully, the Holy Spirit provided insight that I needed to just give this child extra hugs, a little more discipline, and some verbal encouragement, and before long his attitude made a major shift.

Another priceless gift we have in God's presence is that He is our **Comforter.** In Acts 9, Paul talks about "going on in the fear of the Lord and in the comfort of the Holy Spirit . . . " (vs. 31). 2 Corinthians 1 also speaks of the comfort we receive from God, saying that "just as the sufferings of Christ are ours in abundance, so also our comfort is abundant through Christ" (vs. 5). While we are not necessarily suffering to the degree many on earth are, there is certainly a level of suffering that motherhood and simply life brings. But we have a Comforter, one who provides His comfort in abundance. So when we are feeling sad, lonely, or overwhelmed, we must remember that God is near, and that He is there to bring us comfort in all that life throws at us. I have had moments where I was in tears because of the challenges motherhood has brought me. But I am so thankful that God has met me in those moments and been such a comforter. Knowing how deeply He loves me and cares for me is one of the greatest gifts in the world!

God,
Thank You for Your presence. It is our most valuable possession in life. Help us to remember that You are always near, and that You will help, counsel, and comfort us at every turn. Let us walk through our day as moms leaning on You and being led by Your Holy Spirit.
Amen.

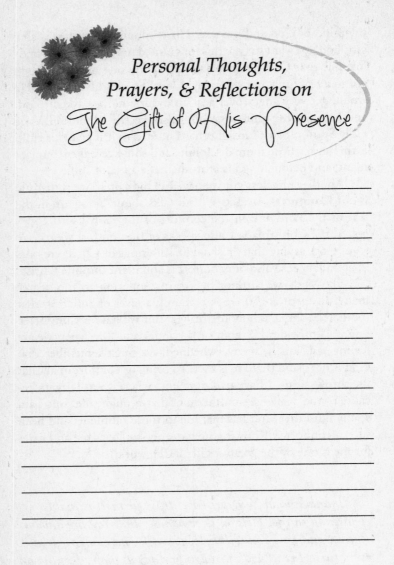

Personal Thoughts,
Prayers, & Reflections on

The Gift of His Presence

"You will make known to me the path of life;
in Your presence is fullness of joy; in Your
right hand there are pleasures forever."

Psalm 16:11

Chapter 3

THE GIFT OF COURAGE

While it takes courage and faith as a mom to get out of bed most days, it also takes courage to walk as the mothers God has called us to truly be. I have been learning this lesson recently as I have begun to recognize that there are so many moments that God is asking me to take courageous action in my mothering, yet I am tempted to be lazy and turn away from the challenge.

The best way I can describe this reality is by explaining my life with my second child, my daughter Hope. She is a born leader, and it started becoming apparent around age two that this little girl wanted to take over the world! While I believe most children are wired with a drive to fight to get their way, this particular child of mine is on continuous overdrive. It is enough to make most people—even most adults—put up their hands in surrender and simply follow her lead.

Yet God has called me to *mother* this child. In other words, I am supposed to lead her, shape her, discipline her, teach her, protect her, and be her benevolent authority. It is a scary calling, and one that I sometimes get insecure about. The truth is, I often feel terribly inadequate and ill-equipped.

She is the type that turns a simple task like brushing her hair into as much work as writing a term paper. I can't count the number of moments I have just felt like giving up and have wondered, "is it really worth it? Is it really *worth* getting her to brush her hair when it is so much *work* for ME?!"

And God continually reminds me that it isn't about her hair (most days we just don't even go there). It is about her heart. It is about helping this precious daughter of mine learn to first be led so that one day she can be a godly leader instead of a tyrant. It is about me being courageous enough to stand up and follow through with what I say, no matter how excruciating it may be. It is about me laying down my fears and my inadequacies and knowing that God alone is my strength and provision.

So in this process I am learning courage. I am realizing God is giving me courage to tackle each challenge my children present to me instead of running from it and burying my head in the sand. I am learning that if I will look to Him and apply Joshua 1:9, "Have I not commanded you? Be strong and courageous! Do not tremble or be dismayed, for the Lord your God will be with you wherever you go" (one of our memory verses we say with the kids), He will give me strategies for how to walk wisely as a mom.

One such strategy has been to give my children plenty of freedom but within boundaries. Choices are such a big deal in today's parenting culture. I think there is some merit to choices, but it is often overdone. Too many choices for younger children can be very overwhelming. Often God shows me to give my children the freedom to choose only between obedience or disobedience. I don't physically force them to obey, but if they choose to disobey, they need to have appropriate consequences. This is where courage really comes in. I have to have the courage to follow through with the consequence even if it is going to mean dealing with a tantrum or a very upset child.

The need for courage in motherhood is constant, whether we realize it or not. For some of us, courage is needed when we have to put our foot down and say no to a contentious toddler. For other moms, the need for courage will come when they have to have a difficult talk with a teen that they keep putting off, or when they have to send them off to college for the first time.

Or what about when one of your children want to go on a mis-sions trip to a war-torn third-world country? No matter what the scenario, the point is that motherhood can be a little scary sometimes. Having responsibility for others' lives is no small job. But God wants to give us moms a gift in this intimidating job . . . the gift of courage as we look to Him to be our strength and to provide what we need to accomplish the work He has set before us to do.

God,
Thank You that You give me the power I need to accomplish
this task of being a mom. Help me to engage in the work
and to not shrink back. Give me courage and strength to
face the many challenges that come my way, and teach me to
lean on You to be my source for it.
Amen.

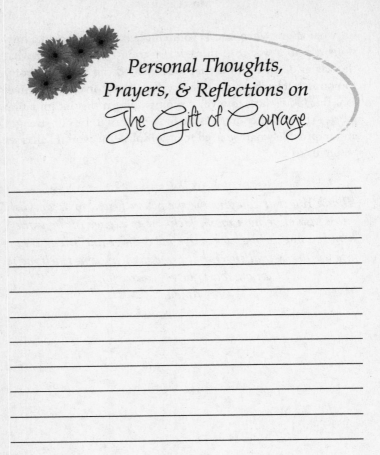

Personal Thoughts,
Prayers, & Reflections on
The Gift of Courage

_____

_____

_____

_____

_____

_____

_____

_____

_____

_____

_____

_____

_____

_____

_____

_____

"Be strong and let your heart take courage,
all you who hope in the Lord."

Psalm 31:24

Chapter 4

THE GIFT OF HOPE

We all have certain strengths and weaknesses as moms, and we do not need to be ashamed of this. The more I have embraced and learned to be real about not only my weaknesses but also my strengths, the easier I have found growth on my journey to be.

One of my personal strengths is hope. God has given me an ability to look toward the future with a strong hope. Some would say I am unrealistic, and perhaps that is true, but I believe that it has more to do with living in hope than anything. What I mean by this is that I have learned how to look ahead with a positive expectation of God's goodness. I have learned that when I am having a hard day, week, or even year, this too shall pass and a new season will come. I believe that my best days are yet ahead, and that God is doing a good work in me and will be faithful to complete it (Philippians 1:6).

My daughter Hope has given me such a clear picture of what hope means. Her name is very fitting for her, as she lives in a perpetual state of hope—always holding on to the 'hope' of things being favorable for her. One of her favorite words is "maybe" because she can't quite be reconciled to the word "no." Her hope is still lacking maturity, but she has the right idea. She understands the goodness of God and is always full of the hope that good things are ahead for her!

The Psalmist says in Psalm 71, "But as for me, I will hope continually. I will praise You yet more and more." God wants us to live in a perpetual state of hope. When we lose site of hoping in God, we quickly sink into a pit of despair and that is no place to operate from as a mom leading our children. Hope is our anchor, and helps us to stay steady and strong. Hebrews 6:18b-19 tells us ". . . we who have taken refuge would have strong encouragement to take hold of the hope set before us. This hope we have as an anchor of the soul, a hope both sure and steadfast and one which enters within the veil . . . " and Hebrews 10:23 similarly encourages us, "Let us hold fast the confession of our hope without wavering, for He who promised is faithful."

Hope is essential to motherhood because it leads us to trust that God is faithful and that we will one day reap a harvest from all that we have sown. I believe motherhood, especially in the early years, is a lot like gardening. We have this garden (our children), and we are sowing seeds into their lives —seeds of love, of teaching and training, of compassion, of time and service. We are weeding the garden as well—disciplining our children in order to see the fruit of righteousness spring up in their lives. Yet so often for me, it has felt as though I am sowing in so much, watering so much, and weeding so much, but there has not been much fruit so far.

That is when hope has to step in. I have to believe that God is faithful and that these seeds I am sowing, this water I am giving, and this weeding I am doing will one day pay off. It doesn't mean it will look exactly like I want, but it does mean that as I hope in God, I will be able to rest in His promises and His faithfulness. It also means that I can persevere and look forward to the fruit that will come as I wait eagerly upon *Him* to bring it, just as Paul encourages us, "For in hope we have been saved, but hope that is seen is not hope; for who hopes for what he already sees? But if we hope for what we do not see, with perseverance we wait eagerly for it" (Romans 8:24-25).

Back to my daughter Hope again—she has been a very real picture of the need to live in hope for my children. As amazing as she is, being the mom of such a strong, determined personality has been excruciatingly hard. Yet God has filled me with such a strong hope and vision for who He has created her to be. I can't wait to see the woman of God she will become one day. She is going to radically change the world! And all of the challenges will become so worth it.

God,
You are the God of hope. Help me to abound in hope by the
power of the Holy Spirit, and to remember always that You
are faithful and You will complete what You have begun.
Give me the strength and hope to persevere in the mundane
tasks of motherhood, knowing that one day I will reap a
bountiful harvest.
Amen.

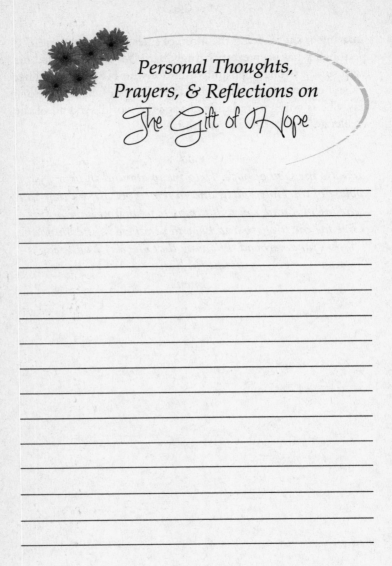

Personal Thoughts,
Prayers, & Reflections on
The Gift of Hope

"Now may the God of hope fill you with all joy
and peace in believing, so that you will abound
in hope by the power of the Holy Spirit."

Romans 15:13

Chapter 5

THE GIFT OF PEACE

G od's gracious gift of peace is a peace that is independent of circumstances. It is not based on our surroundings, which are rarely if ever peaceful as moms. It is a peace that comes solely from above, from the Prince of Peace Himself.

I have found that my ability to keep in perfect peace is in direct correlation with how much I am trusting and resting in Jesus. There are so many times that fear or worry can try to overtake us; many situations vie for our undoing. I'm sure every mother could make her own list of worries, but for the sake of making this practical, I will share a few current personal struggles that fight against my peace.

- The child that is continuously whining any time he doesn't get his way.

- The other child that has to be told five times to do just about anything.

- The *other* child that has a learning disability and is needing an extra amount of help in his schooling as a result.

- The rising cost of food and gas and the new cavities that have to be filled, and the lack of funds in the bank to pay for all of this.

- The three loads of laundry waiting to be done.

- The dryer that is broken and greatly impeding our laundry progress.

- The bathroom that needs to be cleaned.

- The marriage that needs attention and the lack of time available to give it.

- The kitchen that needs to be cleaned and the dinner that needs to be cooked.

- The health concerns that I need to find time to address.

- The child that still needs to learn how to read.

And the list goes on and on. Where is the hope for peace? Praise God, it is not found in my circumstances and it is not dependent on everything working out perfectly. I can have a peace that cannot be shaken, a peace that surpasses understanding.

A verse I love says, "The steadfast of mind You will keep in perfect peace, because he trusts in You." (Isaiah 26:3) There is a definite secret weapon when it comes to staying in perfect peace, and that secret is trust. When we are trusting in Jesus, no matter what circumstances we may find ourselves in, we can stay in a place of peace. We can know that He will take care of us and that we do not have to worry or fret. The other part of this verse is about being steadfast of mind. The question is, what am I dwelling on? If I am mulling over my list of problems and little stresses of life, I will not have peace. But if I am instead focusing on Jesus and His glory and power, the problems will fade into the background. I can remain in God's peace because my eyes are on the One big enough to handle it all.

There are so many things in life that we can worry about, but worry is never productive nor part of Kingdom living. At one point God even showed me how worry is sin, because it is a definite sign that we are not trusting Him. We need to realize we have a Father in heaven who cares for us infinitely more than we even care for our own children. And He is also infinitely more capable of taking care of us and giving us what we need if only we will let Him.

God wants to give us the gift of peace that surpasses under-standing, and He has shown us in His word another secret to receiving this. Philippians 4:6-7 says,

> *"Be anxious for nothing, but in everything by prayer and supplication with thanksgiving let your requests be made known to God. And the peace of God, which surpasses all comprehension, will guard your hearts and your minds in Christ Jesus."*

So really, it is pretty straightforward and simple. If I want God's peace to guard my heart and mind, all I have to do is give up anxious living and instead pray and ask God for what I need. And I need to remember to do it from a place of giv-ing thanks.

I know it is more easily said than done. Life is full of "stresses" that seek to steal our peace. We live in a fallen world that is full of troubles and we are raising humans that are born into sin and cause all manner of difficulties for us. Despite this, I do believe that it is a gift worth fighting for, not only for our own sakes, but also in order that we might be examples to our children of how to live in peace in the midst of a fallen world.

When I am about to go crazy from hearing the whining or fighting, I know I need to tap into the peace that surpasses understanding. Usually it means taking a deep breath and cry-ing out to God in my heart to help me. When I am feeling overwhelmed by the lack of time or money or energy to meet the demands of my children and life, I bring it to God in prayer and begin to thank Him that He is Jehovah Jireh, the Lord my Provider. I also recall and give thanks for His faithfulness to me in the past and for all He has blessed me with in the present. Then suddenly peace is not so far away anymore; instead it is right there with me. His name is Jesus, the Prince of Peace.

So the next time you find yourself in an anxious state and wonder why peace is eluding you, catch yourself. Take the time to go before God and pray. Seek Him, and give thanks to Him for all He is and all He's given you, and present your requests to Him, knowing He hears and cares. Then experience peace come over you like a blanket, enveloping you in His love and tender care. What a precious gift His peace is, and how blessed we are when we open our hearts and minds to receive it!

God,
Thank You for Your peace that surpasses understanding and
that is not based on my earthly circumstances. You are truly
a God of peace, and I desire to trust You with my whole
heart and allow You to guard my heart and my mind.
Teach me how to lay down my anxious thoughts and to live
a life of peace and thanksgiving.
Amen.

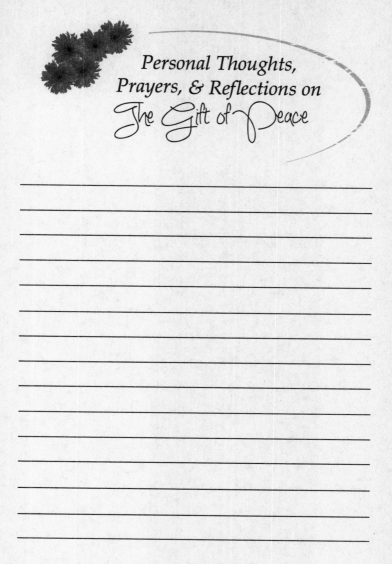

Personal Thoughts, Prayers, & Reflections on
The Gift of Peace

_____

_____

_____

_____

_____

_____

_____

_____

_____

_____

_____

_____

_____

_____

_____

"Peace I leave with you; My peace I give to you;
not as the world gives do I give to you. Do not let
your heart be troubled, nor let it be fearful."

John 14:27

Chapter 6

THE GIFT OF JOY

God has given me a promise of joy for many years now, and it is a promise available to all believers. Yet in my life there has been a specific attack against my joy even since I was a child. For some unknown reason that I still don't understand, depression and sadness had always seemed to be nearer companions than joy. Worry and anxiety were much more familiar. I have had one of the hardest times writing this chapter, because so often I feel as though joy alludes me and I cannot seem to grasp it and hold onto it long enough to understand what it fully means.

Yet there is a joy that is much greater than just happiness, which is not dependent on our emotions or our circumstances. This is the joy that I want to live in and daily walk out. I have found a secret in scripture that tells of the true source of joy. Psalm 16:11 says, "You will make known to me the path of life; *in Your presence is fullness of joy;* in Your right hand there are pleasures forever." Similarly, Psalm 21:6 says, "For You make him most blessed forever; You make him *joyful with gladness in Your presence.*" So it appears that the secret of our joy is found in another gift that He has already given to us! It is in the gift of His presence. There in that place is where the fullness of joy lies.

It often feels too easy to be a grumpy mom. It is never hard to find something to complain about, whether it is how tired we are or how messy the house is or how difficult the children are being. It is easy to get caught in a place of self-pity or to feel just plain grouchy. Whether we are hormonal or genuinely upset about something, these emotions are far too near and ready to embrace us at the slightest glance of our hearts.

Yet there is a gift from God waiting to be unwrapped by each of us. It is a gift of joy; a gift that comes from being in His presence. And because in a sense we are *always* in His presence (Matthew 28:20, John 14:16-17), the gift is accessed from becoming more *aware* of His presence in our lives. The unveiling of our eyes to see Him and behold His beauty (Psalm 27:4) is the source of this joy that is meant to dramatically altar our perspective and attitude. It is even meant to transform our emotions—to lift them off the ground, where they are being dragged around in the mud, and to set them up above in heavenly places, where we are filled with a supernatural joy that doesn't make any worldly sense!

When the foundation for our joy is God and His presence, we can learn how to live in continuous joy no matter what is going on around us. We can also get really good at enjoying and delighting in our children. My three-year-old is definitely one of the funniest and most entertaining people in the world. She says some of the craziest things. Just the other day she said to someone, "I am the mom and you are a pizza." Then the girl said to her, "What are you going to do?" to which she replied (while holding a fork and knife in her hand), "I am going to cut you." She is a crazy child and this is a little on the scary side, but who can help but laugh!? She told another girl, "My eyes are hurting because I have been looking at you. Because your eyes are brown and mine are blue." She also made up a song once that said, "My mom is a lettuce, I don't care, I don't care" because I eat a lot of vegetables and lettuce. She brings us all so much joy, and the amazing thing is that Joy is her middle name!

In recent months I have also learned how to laugh in the midst of some of the most frustrating circumstances. My children have very conflicting personalities and have become experts at fighting and arguing with one another—it seems to be their favorite activity. Sometimes it is maddening to listen to and almost impossible to stop, but as I have grown at remaining in God's presence and joy, He has been empowering me to often smile and laugh in the midst of these episodes rather than scream and pull my hair out. I have been able to delight in them as I watch their intense personalities come out and the things they make into such a big deal, like the fact that one person got one more blueberry than the others. In some of these little ways I am learning how to walk in more joy as a mom, no matter what is happening around me.

Jesus endured the cross for the joy set before Him (Hebrews 12:2). I truly believe that in our mothering, we can endure the challenges and trials for the joy set before us as well. Though it is small in comparison to what Christ endured, we are enduring—for but a brief moment—the trials and tribulations of raising children. In the end, we will have poured out our all and hopefully get to experience the joy of seeing them become mature adults who are lovers of God and people. And the joy that will bring will make it all worth it.

May we all seek out the ultimate Joy-Giver, and learn how to receive this gift He desires to give us in our motherhood. And may we joyously embrace this high-calling of raising our children and giving our all for His sake and theirs.

God,
Thank You for being a joy-giver. Truly it is in Your presence
that we find fullness of joy. Help me to seek You and to
become more aware of Your presence in my life, and in the
process to be filled with a supernatural joy
no matter what is going on around me.
Amen.

Personal Thoughts,
Prayers, & Reflections on

The Gift of Joy

_____

_____

_____

_____

_____

_____

_____

_____

_____

_____

_____

_____

_____

_____

_____

_____

_____

"But let all who take refuge in You be glad, let them
ever sing for joy; and may You shelter them, that
those who love Your name may exult in You."

Psalm 5:11

Chapter 7

THE GIFT OF SEASONS

Motherhood often feels monotonous to me. While nothing is really ever predictable about it, there are so many things that never seem to change. Take the laundry for example. No matter how much I accomplish on one particular day, the clothes pile just grows right back. If I take even one day off, it seems like Mt. Washmore starts to grow so big it may take over the house.

Or what about eating? I have joked countless times about how I am going to impose a fast on my children, just so I can get some sort of a vacation. They never, and I repeat, NEVER stop eating! At one point it seemed that we were spending our entire day in the kitchen just eating, cleaning up, and then preparing for the next meal!

And then there are the other tasks: getting children cleaned up, dressed, teeth and hair brushed, etc. So much of parenting seems to consist of the routine work of meeting basics needs—nothing glamorous, nothing exciting.

Yet within this monotony, God has given us a gift in motherhood: seasons. While we see this in the natural seasons of the earth, there is a special seasonal nature to motherhood that helps break up the monotony and bring refreshment and hope to our lives. When I first began to realize and embrace this reality in my motherhood, I was empowered to receive a new grace God was giving.

The reality is we are in a very seasonal period of life. While all of life consists of different seasons and eras, motherhood has a particularly unique seasonal aspect to it. Just take pregnancy as an example. In my life, I have been pregnant for approximately nine months, every two to three of the last ten years. And when I am pregnant, everything changes for me: what I eat, what I wear, what I think about, how I spend my time, etc. Even my ability to connect with God is different. In fact, my life is so different when I am pregnant that I can't even read the types of books I normally enjoy. I usually read Christian growth books, or books on motherhood, or homeschooling, or other informational books. But when I am pregnant, my brain operates so differently that I can only really read fiction!

I have also been nursing an infant or toddler for most of those ten years. It has meant that I am rarely able to get out and have alone time or leave overnight. This requires the sacrifice of thinking about my baby first because he/she is dependent on me for nurture and sustenance. And while we want to have more children, I have to remember that this season will not last forever, and I should enjoy it while it lasts. It really is such a special time to have that bond with my little one, and it will be a bittersweet day when I wean my last baby and that season of my life comes to a close.

Now that I have had my fifth baby, my perspective is so different. Even though one might think that I would be tired of having babies and going through that newborn or crawling baby season, I am starting to experience the truth of the older moms' advice, "Enjoy this season. It goes by so fast." I have made a conscious effort to delight in this baby so much more as I embrace the season God has me in with him. I have started to understand how quickly time goes by and how brief some of these seasons actually are.

There are so many seasons in motherhood. After the baby and toddler season is over (that potty training season sure was fun!), you get to enjoy the preschool years where they are learning so much every day and working on becoming more independent. Then come the elementary school years where it seems they go from being a little kid to a big kid really fast! Then the preteen years hit and the next thing you know they are in high school! And it only seems like the blink of an eye and they are graduating from high school and are out on their own! In the midst of these seasons, there are things like the holiday season, the summer vacation season, the soccer season, and the high-gear school year season. Within each of these wonderful times that break up the monotony of our daily lives, God gives us so many special gifts.

Sometimes part of the gift is the fact that the season will end. When one of my children is going through a "season" that might be particularly challenging, hope is what I need. I need to be able to place my hope in Jesus, knowing He is with me and that one day this too shall pass. It doesn't mean something else challenging isn't around the corner, but it does mean that I can look to tomorrow with hope that God will see me through this challenge, and will also meet me in the ones ahead.

When my three-year-old entered a season of refusing to nap and go to bed at night, it quickly became an exhausting struggle that went on for days, weeks, months, and eventually more than a year. But then somehow, over the course of a few months, it slowly began to subside and now we are totally past it. It is a faint and distant memory (thank You, God!), and I rarely if ever think about it. We've moved on to other struggles now, like getting this child to not ignore me every time I ask him to do something. However, when a faint memory of that season crosses my mind, I am overwhelmed with thankfulness that God got us through to the other side. Then I try to remember that the challenges I am facing right now will one day be over too.

I want to learn how to embrace and enjoy each season God has me in. Whether it is a season of slowing down so much that we hardly ever go anywhere (a recent season we were just in), or a time of focusing on breaking some bad habits that have developed (like not picking up after ourselves), there are gifts in each one. It is our job to embrace those gifts and realize that though there are hard things in them, there are also hidden blessings. And if nothing else, I believe it is one of God's gracious ways of breaking up some of the more monotonous aspects of motherhood and for that I am grateful.

God,
Thank You for instating seasons into the earth and into our lives. Thank You for the many gifts that each season holds in our lives as moms. Help me to embrace the season I am currently in and to enjoy it fully. Help me to learn all I need to learn, and to remember that both the current blessings as well as the struggles won't last forever.
Amen.

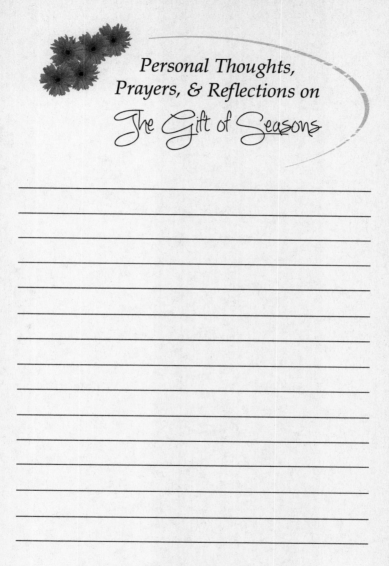

Personal Thoughts,
Prayers, & Reflections on

The Gift of Seasons

_____

_____

_____

_____

_____

_____

_____

_____

_____

_____

_____

_____

_____

_____

_____

"There is an appointed time for everything.
And there is a time for every event under heaven."

Ecclesiastes 3:1

Chapter 8

THE GIFT OF MOMENTS

Babies and young children don't do time changes well. They don't read the clock and tell themselves, "Oh, it's only six o'clock, not seven o'clock." They still get tired and wake up at the same time as they did yesterday. And the funny thing is, the time change everyone gets so excited about is the one that is the hardest for moms! While everyone else is rejoicing over that extra hour of sleep, the kids are now getting up an hour earlier (at least by the clock) than they were the day before. So while others are sleeping in, mom is waking at six instead of seven!

Currently my eighteen-month-old is still having lingering affects from the time change that occurred four days ago. She is now getting up around six in the morning (which used to be seven o'clock) and wanting to start her day. Which means I am up, while the rest of the house is soundly sleeping.

So I have a choice to make. I can either get bitter and bummed that I am having to get up an hour earlier, or I can see it as a gift; an opportunity, a chance to spend some quality morning time with my sweet little girl who is more chipper this time of day than any other. (Plus I get the added benefit of a little quiet time before the rest of the rowdier kids get up).

Many gifts are a choice in perspective, and the gift of these little moments happen all day long in motherhood. But the question is, will we embrace them or pass them by? So often we push them aside in the name of productivity and busyness.

Here is what they look like: a child coming down early in the morning to tell me about a dream he had; my little girl telling me a long and extravagant made up story; a toddler wanting me to hold him after he gets an owie; my teenager actually wanting to tell me about his day; my five-year-old wanting to dance or do a play for me; the baby dancing to the music playing; the funny quip the three-year-old just said (did you catch it?). They happen fast, so fast it is easy to miss them. Yet each of those brief moments of joy, laughter, and relationship, are the substance of life. And beholding them is essential.

It requires a little bit of sacrifice to receive the gifts of moments. We have to hold our own time and agenda loosely. So many times my children are trying to tell me something and I am lost in my own thoughts or busy working on a task. It is hard to stop and give them the attention they deserve. But each time I don't stop, I miss out on the gift God wanted to give me in that moment. I am actually choosing to be about myself instead of my children, and in the process missing a gift.

God gives us so many gifts throughout every day, and many of them are in the mundane routine interactions we have with one another. Yet so often we don't even stop long enough to notice them, much less enjoy them and give thanks. It is usually not until they are gone that we appreciate them.

I'm sure we've all experienced those older mothers telling us to enjoy our children when they are young because it goes so fast. Though we know that what they are saying is true, it is usually hard to fully receive it, because we are in the thick of the challenges. Even if we are able to feel nostalgic for a moment, the fight that breaks out over who had the crayon first instantly jars us back into reality. Yet we desperately want to heed the warning from these moms. We don't want to end up with regrets.

May we embrace each gift with wide-open arms, and not miss it. Let's just leave the dishes in the sink sometimes and the email in the inbox, and watch as the baby tries to walk, the toddler blows bubbles in the yard, or the older ones perform a play. Or better yet, let's jump in and join them.

Several times lately I have joined my children jumping on the trampoline, mainly with the intention of getting a little exercise. Little did I know that God really wanted to just give me the gift of a moment. My children think it is as exciting as a birthday party when mom comes and jumps on the trampoline with them. Everyone in the family comes out and jumps together when I get in there! We run around and laugh and get filled with so much joy together.

A moment. Did I take it in? Did I receive the gift? It was brief, and there is no guarantee we will all be here tomorrow to repeat it. So I am learning how to stop in the midst of a hundred things to do, breathe deeply, and receive the gift of each moment He gives me with these dear ones.

God,
You give us hundreds of gifts each day. Thank You for all
the little moments of blessing You desire us to unwrap
throughout our day as a mom. Help us to slow down long
enough to open these gifts and to take them in. Give us
Your perspective to see how precious these fleeting moments
with our children are.
Amen.

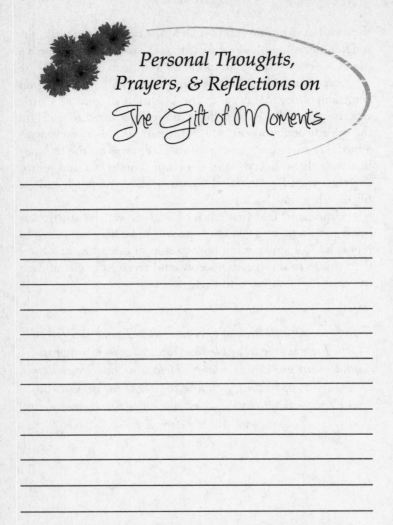

Personal Thoughts,
Prayers, & Reflections on

The Gift of Moments

_____

_____

_____

_____

_____

_____

_____

_____

_____

_____

_____

_____

"Lord, make me to know my end and what is the
extent of my days; let me know how transient I am.
Behold, You have made my days as handbreadths,
and my lifetime is as nothing in Your sight; surely
every man at his best is a mere breath. Selah."

Psalm 39:4-5

Chapter 9

THE GIFT OF REST

Being given the gift of rest in motherhood sounds like an oxymoron. However, it is not the kind of rest the world knows. It is not laying on the beach, soaking up the rays and listening to the waves crash on the shore. It is not sleeping in late. It is not a quiet, peaceful, lazy morning sitting on the porch with a cup of tea. It is a deeper and more profound rest; a rest that remains regardless of circumstances. It is a rest that cannot be shaken and is only found in surrender to Jesus, who said, "Come to Me, all who are weary and heavy-laden, and I will give you rest" (Matthew 11:28).

He offers an invitation. It is simple, yet profound—COME. The secret to rest is coming to Him. In this coming, there is also the chance to surrender it all and lay everything at His feet; like those fears that keep us up at night, the suffocating worries from the weight we carry, the overwhelming anxiety of having to hold it all together. We have to give it all over to Him and trust.

In this process, I have begun to find rest. Even on days when my sum total of sleep, though broken up three times, is only four or five hours. Even when all chaos has broken loose in my house because the dog threw up all over the carpet in the middle of the night and everyone is screaming because they are hungry but also tired and need a nap. Even though there is only one of me and fifteen things that need to be done in the next five minutes, rest can still be my reality. Yet I must COME. And I must lean heavy on the only One big enough and strong enough to carry all that is on my plate. As I clean up the dog vomit and try to calm the screaming children, I can supernaturally tap into this peace by COMING to Jesus in my heart and crying out to Him for His peace.

There is a need as moms to learn how to come to Jesus in the midst of busyness. We usually can't stop what we are doing and get away to a quiet room by ourselves to find His peace (though we can get really good at taking advantage of bathroom trips and shower times). But just because we can't get away to a quiet place does not mean we cannot *come to Jesus* in our hearts and minds. We have to discipline our minds to keep our thoughts on Him and discipline our hearts to remain in Him. This is the secret to our peace and rest. While it might seem abstract at times, it is very real and practical in many ways. It is the secret of the abiding life and of knowing how to live and breathe and have our very being in Him.

While it is so easy to succumb to, there is really no room for striving in motherhood, or we will collapse under the weight of it all. I have never experienced something that delivers such a large amount of sustained pressure on a daily basis as motherhood does. If I try to go it alone, by sheer will and determination, I will most certainly implode. Yet if I will lay it all down and choose to let Jesus be my burden bearer, the same amount of pressure that could cause my demise will instead be the instrument God will use to produce fine jewels in my life. Rubies and many other beautiful gems are made from the pressure of the rocks in the earth. This process somehow produces the jewel, and God does the same in our lives if we will let Him. So the pressure of motherhood can be given to Jesus and bring forth jewels, or we can try to go it alone and be turned into volatile volcanoes.

We must learn the secret of resting in Jesus, and trusting Him in the midst of the chaos. He is a very real and present help to us and His rest is available. May we learn to come and receive His rest no matter what is happening all around us.

God,
Thank You that You are our resting place. Thank You
that You offer a real rest that is not dependent on our
surroundings or circumstances. Teach me how to come to
You and receive rest for my often weary soul. I find rest in
You alone and I need it so badly. May I not strive and fight,
but simply trust and receive the rest You desire to give me.
Amen.

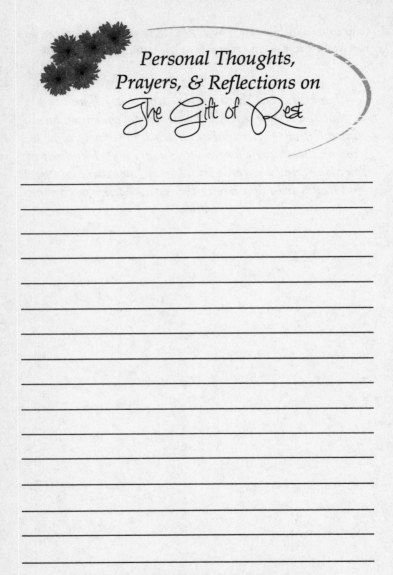

Personal Thoughts,
Prayers, & Reflections on
The Gift of Rest

_____

_____

_____

_____

_____

_____

_____

_____

_____

_____

_____

_____

_____

_____

_____

_____

"Come to Me, all who are weary and heavy-
laden, and I will give you rest."

Matthew 11:28

Chapter 10

THE GIFT OF DEPENDENCE

While a close relative of rest, dependence is still deserving of its own chapter, as it is the crucible of learning the secret of success in life, as well as in motherhood. If we want to experience grace in our lives, learning to live a life of dependence on the Father, Son, Holy Spirit, and the family of God is essential.

There is no room for independent living in the Kingdom of God. Isolation and an "I can do it all myself" attitude is a one-way ticket to certain demise. I have experienced the radical gift of learning to be dependent on God and others, and I know one massive way He has taught me this has been through getting me in over my head through my children!

I often feel like God has completely set me up to learn humility and dependence. It seems He has given me children that are exceptionally intense. God has given us a whole brood of strong-willed leaders that desperately want to be in charge. Ultimately I see it as a good thing, but raising leaders is full of challenges! On top of that, we also live in the midst of a very busy church community where ministry is going on around us all of the time. Our home is the hub for a lot of college students that are in and out every day, and in various seasons we have had a lot of church meetings, including our Sunday gatherings, happening at our house. We often have teams of people from out-of-town churches come through and stay at our house as well. The revolving door plus the normal daily challenges of having five kids and homeschooling them, has made for some pretty overwhelming situations.

In addition to what often seems like an exceptionally busy life, I have been blessed with the added "asset" of being a particularly disorganized and slow person. My personality is a bit all over the place, and while I have a higher tolerance than most for chaos, it is certainly not my preference. Unfortunately, structure, consistency, and follow-through are not my strong points. On top of that, I find it so interesting that God would call me to a life of such fullness and also create me as a slower-than-normal person. I am ultimately the one responsible for the dishes, laundry, cleaning, cooking, homeschooling, shopping, etc., and yet it seems to always take me twice as long as the average person to get them done. The only thing I have been able to make of this situation is that God really wanted me to be able to learn how to depend on Him and others.

Thankfully, He has provided a lot of help. He is my ultimate Helper, and the One I put my trust in to meet every need. He has also provided many human helpers as well. Over the years many of the students in our ministry have volunteered to come and help around our home and with our children. I know I could not carry the weight of it all without them and their gracious help. When our fifth baby was born, God provided an amazing intern all the way from England to come be a part of our church community and help our family!

I am continuously amazed at just how much help I need. There are so many days when I stand in the middle of my crazy messy kitchen thirty minutes before I need to have dinner ready and just want to cry. Not only do I not know what I am making yet, but I can't even find a spot to chop up a zucchini if I wanted to. So, I cry out to God, "HELP me!" He calms me down, and I realize He is faithful and dependable and will help me to get done what I need to do. I just need to take action, and watch Him faithfully meet my needs. I also know some of the help I need is to learn how to be more organized and implement structures and systems that work better. Even right now He has provided a good friend to come alongside me and teach me how to implement better systems in my home and with my children. It is amazing how much more gifted she is in the organization and structure department than I am. I have given her permission to speak boldly into my life and to really challenge me to change areas that are not working. It is not going to be an easy journey for me, but I know it will be worth it.

Part of learning dependency is to recognize the areas in our life that we are not good at and be willing to get help with them. We really need to give others a voice into our lives. It is part of breaking off an independent spirit that says, "I've got this. I can handle it and don't need anyone else." Proverbs 12:15 sums it up well, "The way of a fool is right in his own eyes, but a wise man is he who listens to counsel." I am a big fan of learning from others who are more gifted at certain things than me, as well as those who have gone before me and therefore have more experience. I want to gain wisdom from them and prevent unnecessary mistakes. One time God spoke to me out of Proverbs 13:20 which says, "He who walks with wise men will be wise . . . " and at the same time quickened in my heart that a particular older woman I knew was wise. So I invited her over and asked her to observe my daily life at home with my children and to speak into it. It was amazing some of the things she was able to give me insight into and the wisdom she had for me to implement.

While being willing to rely on the help and gifts of others is so important (as opposed to pridefully thinking I can just do it all myself), my greatest need for help isn't even in the practical areas! My greatest need is in the arenas of my heart and mind. There are days when I feel like I am in a war to maintain any sense of peace and sanity. Oh, how I need Jesus just to make it through those days! I love Isaiah 26:3 which says, "The steadfast of mind You will keep in perfect peace, because he trusts in You." When I am struggling to maintain sanity, I always know that my only hope is to stop leaning on myself and to depend on Jesus more fully. When I put my hope and trust in Him and turn my mind to Him, He really does ground me and bring peace. Even when I am standing in the middle of a very messy kitchen and need to figure out what to make for dinner AND cook it in the next ten minutes!

But I want to do more than just survive in life and in motherhood; I want to learn how to thrive. I want to live full of life and joy and in the abundance of all God has for me. I have come to realize that the only way this is going to be possible is for me to live completely dependent on God. If I try to live life apart from Him for even a moment, much less a day, I quickly start to sink. The life of a mom is simply too intense (at least from my experience) to be able to survive, much less thrive, apart from total dependence on God.

God,
Thank You that You are faithful and dependable. Thank
You for desiring that I would learn how to lean on and be
dependent upon You. Help me to not take things into my
own hands and strive to make it work by my own strength.
And help me to be humble enough to accept that I need
help from others too, and to thankfully receive
the help when it is offered.
Amen.

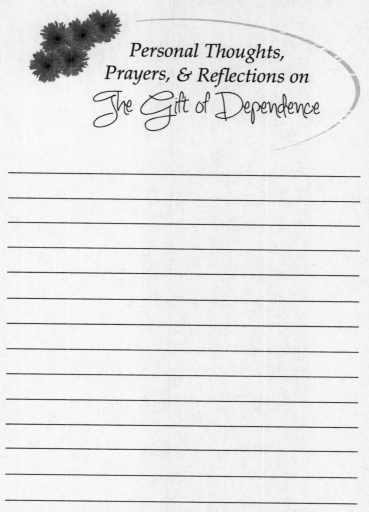

Personal Thoughts,
Prayers, & Reflections on
The Gift of Dependence

_____

_____

_____

_____

_____

_____

_____

_____

_____

_____

_____

_____

_____

"He only is my rock and my salvation, my stronghold;
I shall not be shaken. On God my salvation and my
glory rest; the rock of my strength, my refuge is in
God. Trust in Him at all times, O people; pour out
your heart before Him; God is a refuge for us. Selah."

Psalm 62:7-8

Chapter 11

THE GIFT OF MOM FRIENDS

A really sweet and unexpected gift God has given me in motherhood is my fellow warriors and comrades in the faith-filled journey. I once read in a parenting magazine that nothing gives you such an instant bond with others as becoming a mom. All of a sudden you have more things to talk about with a perfect stranger than you could have ever thought possible. From birth stories to potty training woes to how your baby won't sleep, there are so many things to share about and seek one another's advice on.

Then eventually you start to find that handful of other moms that you really connect with, and you decide to become true friends. You begin to use the excuse of play dates to be able to get together and fellowship with one another. And you soon find that God has a really special gift in the friendships of other moms.

Some days you simply appreciate having an adult conversation with someone, while on other days you are desperate to feel understood. Maybe you are needing some wisdom and advice, or maybe you just need someone to listen compassionately without trying to fix the problem.

I also have loved that God has given me a handful of like-minded moms who get to encourage one another in radical ways as we journey along in motherhood. We can speak into each other's lives and offer insight that we often miss when we are in the midst of it all. God has given me some very special friends who fit this category. Doris McDonnell, Dia Becchio, Kim Zakaryan, April Hoffmann, Melissa Barnett (who is also my sister-in-law!), Jill Schalesky, Melanie Sunukjian, Michelle Ryan, and Becky Jo Cummings all come to mind. And as I think about each of them, I am overwhelmingly thankful for the incredible gift they are in my life. I don't know what I would do without them, and I am amazed at God's goodness to give us one another.

Some of them don't even live near me anymore, and then there are those who are right in town that I get to see on a regular basis. But overall it is just knowing they are all there, in their own homes with their amazing children, fighting the good fight of faith and raising up little warriors, that gives me amazing hope and joy as I do the same thing in my home. Then when we get to enjoy some face-to-face time, my spirit soars as we encourage one another in the deep things of God and motherhood, and are reminded of why we are doing this labor of love and that we are not alone in it.

I wish I had the space to write about each of these dear ones God has given me, but I will pick one for the sake of time and space. Becky Jo has been a particularly sweet and surprising gift of God to me. She is one of the most amazing people I've met, and we are just the right amount of similar and different to be a perfect combo! We were at a family camp near San Diego put on by a very encouraging ministry for wives and mothers called *Above Rubies*. My cool, Southern California husband was a bit skeptical of the whole thing, weary that we were going to be at something with a bunch of Amish-type, awkward homeschooling families. But we pulled up to our cabin and immediately saw our neighbors . . . another totally "normal" looking young family with four children very close in age to ours.

We shared a porch for those two days and somehow, in the midst of taking care of our combined seven kids under the age of seven, God miraculously allowed us to connect with their family in a way that I believe will last for life. Our kids hit it off, our husbands hit it off, and Becky Jo and I practically became best friends. It was amazing to meet another mom who shared so many similarities with me: age, a willingness to have a lot of kids, healthy eating convictions, homeschooling, a creative and laid-back nature, and most of all, a radical lover of Jesus and a woman of faith. What fun it was to meet this amazing person and start to become friends! As we loaded up our cars two days later to drive back to our respective homes that were two-and-a-half hours away from each other, we said we needed to try to visit one another sometime. And somehow we knew we would actually follow through with it.

Since that fateful weekend four years ago, we have somehow managed to visit one another about ten times! We have also added four more children between us, and have become some of each other's best friends. Every time we are together God does something amazing in our hearts, and Becky Jo and I are able to encourage one another and speak into each other's lives in a way few others can. I ask her to tell me ways I need to grow, and she shares honestly, candidly, and encouragingly. God shows us things for one another that He is doing in the seasons we are in, and we are able to speak deeply into one another's lives as wives, mothers, and followers of Jesus. Despite the physical distance we usually have between us, we can call each other to seek out God's perspective in a myriad of circumstances and struggles. It has been such a gift to have this friend that knows me so well and can speak so deeply into my life!

God,
Thank You for the gift of friends. Thank You that I don't
have to be a mom all alone, but that You desire for me to
journey with others. Give me the mom friends You want me
to have and help us to bring amazing encouragement and
support to one another. Help us to learn from one another
and to know how to speak into each other's lives
in a meaningful and edifying way.
Amen.

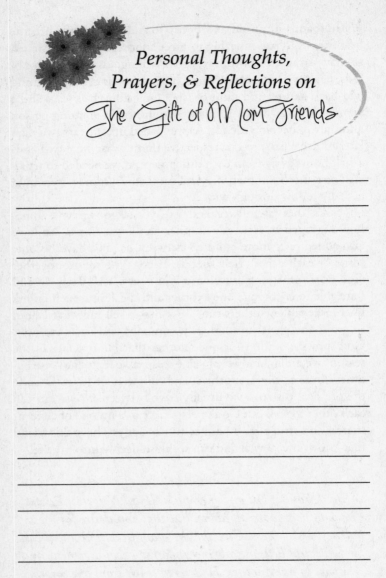

Personal Thoughts,
Prayers, & Reflections on
The Gift of Mom Friends

_____

_____

_____

_____

_____

_____

_____

_____

_____

_____

_____

_____

_____

_____

_____

"Therefore encourage one another and build
up one another, just as you also are doing."

1 Thessalonians 5:11

Chapter 12

THE GIFT OF HUMILITY

There is something about motherhood that promotes humility in our lives. We are put into a hidden place where our lives consist of about 90 percent completely unglamorous tasks—anyone ever counted how many bottoms they have wiped in a week?—with very little thanks or accolades given. What is there to be proud of really?

Not only that, but we have the opportunity to live out the concept of losing our life in a very real way. In Matthew 16:25, Jesus says, "For whoever wishes to save his life will lose it; but whoever loses his life for My sake will find it." Motherhood is such a great way to learn how to live out this Kingdom truth. We get the constant opportunity to lose our life for the sake of Jesus and His children. We have the privilege of learning that it is not about us, and that it is in laying down our lives that we will truly find them.

Learning how to put others first is essential to a route of freedom in this life of faith. And what better way to learn that then to have children . . . to be given lives to steward, love, and sacrifice for daily. They are so needy and dependent on us and we have the privilege of being the tangible expression of the provision of their needs being met. God is the provider ultimately, but for a child, their provision of love, acceptance, care, nourishment, and so much more comes through their parents.

Having the constant opportunity to put our children first allows us to learn to be free from self-centeredness and pride (close brothers in my opinion). We can't be the center of our lives anymore, because there just isn't the time and space available for it. Needy young ones demand so much more of us than we ever thought we had the capacity for. But as we tap into God to receive what we are needing to give, somehow along the way we begin to get free from our greatest hindrances in life, namely pride and selfishness.

As we begin to realize that it is not about us and start finding our life as we lose it, humility becomes a reality in our lives. Not only does humility become a real substance in us through learning how to sacrifice for the sake of our beloved children, but it also becomes so much more tangible through the daily experience of failure. Maybe this is unique to me, but I have never been called to something that I have felt more poorly equipped for than being a mom. Nothing has ever stretched me as much, tested me as much, or drawn as much out of me as motherhood has. And never has anything revealed more of my weaknesses and selfishness. The dawning of those realities has brought a sober humility into my life in a profound way. I cannot simply pull it all together and be the "perfect mom" that I wish I could be.

If it is not my own impatience keeping me humble, it is the many imperfections of my children. There is a reality to feeling shamed by our children's poor behavior around others. We can't help but experience it as a reflection of us. Not only are they our flesh and blood, but they are also a product of our training and modeling. If they start yelling and throwing a fit out in public, we immediately feel like a failure as a mom. One time I was in the grocery store with only two of my then four children (albiet they were the two particularly rowdy and challenging ones). After an entire shopping experience full of difficulty, they mutinied on me and started literally running and yelling all the way around entire aisles while I was standing in the check out line. I was so embarrassed I honestly kind of pretended they weren't mine. Yet instead of going to a place of shame, I've found God wants to use these many episodes where my children aren't getting it quite right to teach me grace for human weakness and to keep me humble. Thank God He doesn't require perfection from us, so why should I require it of my children? I am so thankful that my children and their imperfections can remind me that we are ALL in such need of Him, and it is not our job to be perfect. It is our job to be dependent, humble, and teachable. It is what I desire for my children, and it is what He desires from me, His daughter.

God,
Thank You for the opportunity to grow in humility through the journey of motherhood. You have provided so richly for me to be aware of my weaknesses and shortcomings, and to know it is You within me that gives me the ability to do this work You've called me to. Help me to humble myself and to receive YOUR grace and power to live this life victoriously. I don't want to make it about myself, so empower me to lay down my life and in the process find it.
Amen.

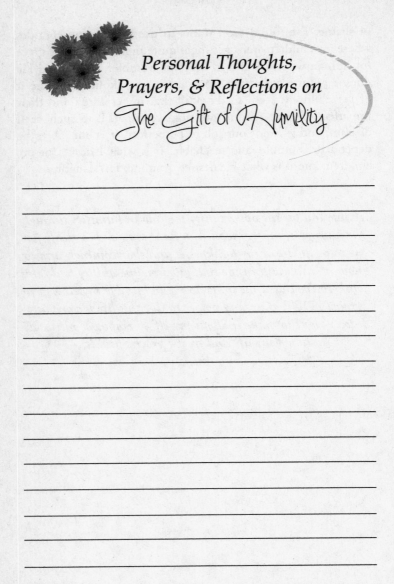

Personal Thoughts,
Prayers, & Reflections on
The Gift of Humility

_____

_____

_____

_____

_____

_____

_____

_____

_____

_____

_____

_____

_____

_____

_____

"But He gives a greater grace. Therefore it says, 'God is
opposed to the proud, but gives grace to the humble.'"

James 4:6

Chapter 13

THE GIFT OF NOURISHING

I truly believe one of the greatest privileges we have as mothers is the gift of being able to nourish our children. We get to provide nourishment for them in a myriad of ways on a daily basis. No other person really gets to have the responsibility for a child the way a mother does. She provides them with sustenance from the day they are born with milk for their growing bodies, as well as eye contact, warmth, cuddles, a reassuring voice, and comfort for their growing minds and spirits. And from there, she makes hundreds of choices as the child grows about what they eat, hear, watch, read, play, and so on.

I love that I get to pour into my children some of the best "food" God has created, not only the rich and wholesome plant and animal foods for their bellies, but also the rich and real food of the Gospel. And it doesn't stop there. I get to nourish their souls as I help walk them through their inner struggles with anger, selfishness, and hurt. And as a homeschooling family, I get to decide how I want to best nourish my children's minds. It is not about trying to control a child or their every circumstance, but it is about the gift God gives us to help nourish their life not only in the physical sense, but also in the emotional, intellectual, and spiritual sense.

Let's briefly look at these four categories of nourishing our children one at a time. We will start with the most obvious—physical nourishment. Though I could write a whole book on this topic (and perhaps one day will), that is not my purpose here, and I don't want to belabor the point. So I will keep it short and sweet. I am known to be a bit obsessive over how I feed my children and my passion for healthy eating. For me, it is something I can't help but do, when I feel so strongly that I have been given these children as gifts to steward. If I love them, which all mothers obviously do, then I of course want what is best for them. So in my mind, if certain foods and qualities of foods are what is best, and are beneficial and health promoting, while others foods are not, I have a hard time not choosing to feed them only the best. For me personally, it has never made sense why I would want my children to put something into their mouths and bodies that will not promote good things in them.

I feel the same way about their hearts. I want to nourish their hearts and spirits with the truths of God's word and the reality of who He is. I want to be intentional in the way I speak about Him and not misrepresent Him because I am having a hard day. Of course, I will behave in ways that are not in line with God's character. So I make sure I communicate to my children what He is like (and even the ways that I fall short in representing this). I want to introduce them to the person of Jesus and allow them to experience His presence and be real in their lives, no matter what age they are. When we water down the Gospel for our children or believe the lie that they can't understand the deep things of God because of their age, I think we often end up giving our children spiritual "junk food." It makes me think of the well-known book by Philip Yancey, *The Jesus I Never Knew*, in which he talks about how the "flannel board Jesus from Sunday school" was such a weak and watered-down version of all that Jesus truly is. It is my desire to protect my children from the Gospel being such a boring religious thing that they want nothing to do with Jesus when they are older. I want to nourish their hearts with the powerful, exciting realities of the Kingdom and of a Savior who loves them more than they can ever imagine!

And so it goes with their souls (the will and emotions) as well. Am I nourishing their souls with the life-giving principles of the Word? Am I shepherding them in a way that empowers them with the life-transforming message of the Gospel, or am I simply trying to control and manage their behavior? As believers and mothers, I think nourishing our children's souls means walking them through the myriad of struggles and emotions they will encounter as they deal with their own anger, selfishness, pain, sadness, etc. Instead of feeding our children's souls "junk food" (which is to slap band-aid answers on their real struggles and emotions), we must help them to see who they really are, righteous and beloved in the sight of God, and in turn teach them to lean on the Holy Spirit to live that out. We must give them a platform to be real on, and then encourage them into their true identities.

I will quickly give an example to illustrate this point. How often as mothers do we deal with the bickering between siblings by quickly forcing them to share, stop fighting, apologize, etc.? We often just try to solve the problem in some poorly thought out way. Nourishing our children's souls means helping them to identify what is going on in their hearts and then shepherding them into a more life-giving way of handling their emotions. "Are you treating your brother the way you would like to be treated?" has been a very effective question in our family. We are not shaming them or forcing compliance, but are helping them to see where they are amiss and how they can make a choice that would be not only more loving and kind, but feel much better to their own souls. Because this is often very challenging to do (for both us and them), we must learn how to lean on the Holy Spirit to guide us and give us insight. I often pray with my children when they are struggling with their emotions, asking God to help them. And I truly do ask God for wisdom for myself as I shepherd them through the maze of their own souls.

Finally, what does it mean to nourish a child's mind?

To me, it is exposing them to truth, real learning, and a rich education, instead of "junk food" for their brains (i.e., fruitless or ungodly input from TV, the internet, games, books, relationships, etc.). I think it is easy for moms to go with the status quo and think that if everyone else is letting their kids watch/read/listen to it, it must be fine for my kids. But we must not be so easily deceived. It is our job as their parents to be aware of what is before our children's eyes and ears, and to do our best to make sure they are things that will nourish their minds rather than dull them.

For our family, homeschooling our children has been a powerful way to invest in nourishing their minds. While I know it is not for everyone, I am a huge fan of homeschooling. It has been a sweet gift that God has given me as I have learned how multi-faceted nourishing my children's minds is. I have loved teaching my children how to learn, and observing how different they each are in that process. I have enjoyed contemplating what is important to teach my children, and what things we can do without. I love that we can learn about the world around us and history through "living" books, hands on experiences, thoughtful discussions, interesting resources, etc. instead of regurgitated textbooks, limited classroom settings, busy work, and a state imposed timetable. Kids truly do have an innate desire to learn. I believe it is our job as mothers to nourish their minds by exposing them to as many interesting and intriguing things to learn about as possible, to pique that interest rather than to dull it.

God,
Thank You for the HONOR of stewarding these children
You have given me. Give me great wisdom to know how to
nourish them in a way that is pleasing to You, body, heart,
soul, and mind. Lead me as I lead them, that we
may all bring You great glory and honor.
Amen.

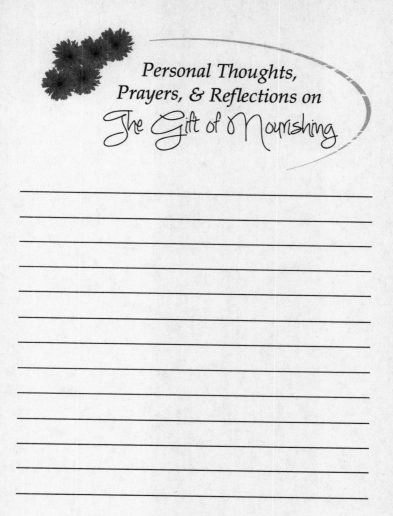

Personal Thoughts, Prayers, & Reflections on

The Gift of Nourishing

_____

_____

_____

_____

_____

_____

_____

_____

_____

_____

_____

_____

"I will feed them in a good pasture, and their
grazing ground will be on the mountain heights
of Israel. There they will lie down on good
grazing ground and feed in rich pasture on the
mountains of Israel. I will feed My flock and I
will lead them to rest,' declares the Lord God."

Ezekiel 34:14-15

Chapter 14

THE GIFT OF PATIENCE

What book on God's gifts in motherhood would be complete without a chapter on patience? A few of these chapters elude me and I feel a bit inadequate to write them. In other words, I am still trying to learn how to receive the gift. Patience is one of those chapters.

Yet I am still astutely aware of the offer of the gift that God so graciously holds out to me on numerous occasions throughout my day. We all know that most of the time if we really want to get good at something, we need to practice; if we want to learn something and have it stick with us, repetition is a must. It seems God has a high value for teaching us patience, as He gives us so many opportunities to learn and grow in it when we are moms.

Where else can we be provided with the opportunity to practice patience in such a consistent and repetitive way then with our children? Whether it is the four-plus years that I have been required to daily remind my daughter to sit down in her chair while she is at the table, or the countless times a day I must tell a child to stop or start doing something, the patience required for this job is limitless.

I found this amazing explanation of patience on Wikipedia (of all places). Some wise person who really had a grasp of the concept wrote, "Patience (or forbearing) is the state of endurance under difficult circumstances, which can mean persevering in the face of delay or provocation without acting on annoyance/anger in a negative way; or exhibiting forbearance when under strain, especially when faced with longer-term difficulties. Patience is the level of endurance one can take before negativity."

If that is not motherhood summed up in so many ways, I don't know what is. Not a day goes by where I am not in need of endurance under difficult circumstances. As a mom, even when I am on vacation, my work goes with me. There are no breaks, and endurance and perseverance is key to my survival. The difficulties I am under are definitely of the longer-term variety, and my need for endurance is a grace I want to grow in so much more.

Yet while I am still very much in process on this one, I can also look back and see just how much patience God has already grown in me, and for this gift I am so grateful. I remember the days when I would get so upset if my first baby would get woken up from a nap by some noise, or when a child was making a mess. Now I have more patience for those things than I do an itch on my back! But it was only through much practice and many opportunities that God brought me to the level of patience I am currently at. And when I continue to experience the myriad of daily opportunities to grow in patience, I want to see those chances as gifts instead of annoyances. For one day I will reap great fruit and will truly have received an abundant gift of patience from my Father's gracious hand.

I also know God wants me to receive this gift of patience for my children, that I might be able to patiently await the work He is doing in them as well. Sometimes I am so impatient as I work to see my children overcome many of their own struggles, be it with selfishness, disobedience, destructive behavior (that's literal, like drawing on walls or ripping up books), fighting, yelling, whining, and the list goes on. But as I am learning how patient God is with me as I grow in my weaknesses and struggles, I am realizing how much more I need to extend this same patience to my children. I want to learn how to recognize the things they HAVE grown out of or improved in, and to rejoice in those, rather than to always focus on the issues they still struggle with. Then I want to trust that God is at work in them and that one day they will not struggle any longer with being able to stay sitting in their seat at the table! Until that day comes, I can embrace the chance to grow in His gift of patience at work within my own life as I learn to calmly and graciously repeat, "Hope, please sit down," ten to fifteen times a day!

God,
Thank You that one of the fruits of the Spirit is patience.
Help me to abide in Your Holy Spirit and let patience be
a fruit in my life. Give me patience throughout the day as
I love and care for my children. Thank You for the many
opportunities You give me to grow in this gift.
Amen.

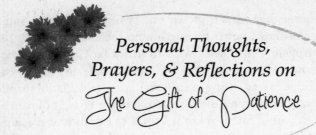

Personal Thoughts,
Prayers, & Reflections on
The Gift of Patience

_____

_____

_____

_____

_____

_____

_____

_____

_____

_____

_____

_____

"Love is patient . . ."
1 Corinthians 13:4

"But the fruit of the Spirit is love, joy, peace, patience . . ."
Galatians 5:22

Chapter 15

THE GIFT OF REFINEMENT

> "And I will bring the third part through the fire, refine
> them as silver is refined, and test them as gold is tested.
> They will call on My name, and I will answer them; I will
> say, 'They are My people,' and they will say,
> 'The Lord is my God.'"

Zechariah 13:9

Perhaps your experience of motherhood has been slightly
different than mine. But I would have to say that I can
liken my experience in many ways to the infamous "refiner's fire" (see Psalm 66:10 and Isaiah 48:10) in which the
silver or gold is heated to high temperatures and the impurities
are brought to the surface in order to be skimmed off the top.
This process leaves the precious metals in a much purer state
and therefore able to shine and glimmer all the more brightly.

It's not that I thought I was perfect before having children, but there just weren't nearly as many catalysts to draw
out all of those impurities still within my heart. It wasn't until I was thrust into the continuous and intense journey of
motherhood that God really turned up the heat in my life,
enough to bring forth so many of those impurities that He
still wanted to skim off the top.

It has been painful to see some of the things still within me. The anger, the impatience, and the selfishness disgust and sadden me. Yet I have learned that God allows me to be in these situations because He loves me and wants me free of these "contaminants."

Oftentimes, I have found that the refining happens without me even realizing it. While I feel the heat, it is not until I look back that I can usually see how He has used it to purify me. Romans 5:3-5 explains an important truth that applies here,

> *"And not only this, but we also exult in our tribulations, knowing that tribulation brings about perseverance; and perseverance, proven character; and proven character, hope; and hope does not disappoint, because the love of God has been poured out within our hearts through the Holy Spirit who was given to us."*

The perseverance through the tribulations have truly brought about a depth of character I could never have gained otherwise. I could share countless examples to illustrate this truth, but one that comes to mind is that every single night my daughter Joanna puts up a huge fuss when I brush her teeth. It has been going on for almost two years now and certainly feels like a source of "heat" in my life. It might not sound like a big deal, but when your two-year old (and then three-year-old) screams bloody murder and acts like she is being beaten the whole time you are simply trying to brush her teeth (unfortunately I am not exaggerating), night after night, week after week, month after month, it is actually an incredibly stressful experience. Yet while it is still frustrating, when I was brushing her teeth tonight I realized how God has used this small nightly struggle to refine me. I have been pressed into greater patience and learning how to persevere through these many types of small daily tribulations. It has produced in me greater character and I barely even flinch at these types of things anymore.

I know He is doing a good work, and that little bit by

little bit, as He keeps that fire blazing, I am truly being refined and purified. Sometimes it doesn't seem that way, but when I look back on the person I was a year ago (much less five), I am amazed at the work He has done. Yet it would not have been accomplished if it was not for that refiner's fire He has allowed me to be placed in, continuously drawing out those impurities and refining who I am, ultimately making me more like Him. For this gift I am eternally grateful.

God,
As painful as the refiner's fire can be at times, I am so
thankful for the chance to be purified and cleansed. Help
me to embrace Your refining process with gratitude and
bring me forth as gold refined by the fire.
Amen.

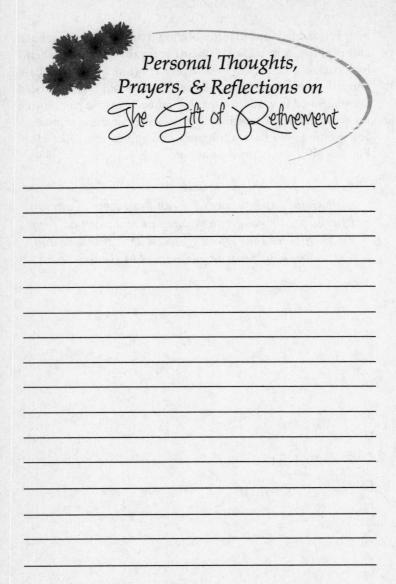

Personal Thoughts,
Prayers, & Reflections on
The Gift of Retirement

_____

_____

_____

_____

_____

_____

_____

_____

_____

_____

_____

_____

_____

_____

_____

_____

"Behold, I have refined you, but not as silver; I
have tested you in the furnace of affliction."

Isaiah 48:10

Chapter 16

THE GIFT OF WISDOM

A s any mom knows, motherhood stretches us in a multitude of ways, many of which we didn't even know were possible. It not only challenges us physically (pregnancy, lack of sleep, carrying babies and toddlers, etc.) and emotionally (joy, sadness, anger, fear, excitement, etc.), but it is also a very mentally stretching experience.

I cannot count the number of times I have felt like I didn't know what to do as a mom. Whether it has been how to go about handling my child's learning disability or how to solve the day after day argument about who sits by me at the breakfast table, I have found that my need for wisdom is relentless.

Is there really any perfect solution on how to handle a child that won't stay in bed? What about parenting those really stubborn children that no amount of discipline seems to effect? Or figuring out how to decide what and how many extracurricular activities to put my children in. How can I know which child will become an artist and needs to be in art class or which one needs to do soccer and baseball? When I am faced with a problem that seems to have no clear answer, I have repeatedly learned that I serve a God who is wise beyond all others, whose wisdom far surpasses our greatest understanding.

For example, when my third child was about eight-months-old, he had developed a horrible habit of screaming to communicate at the table. To get more food or to express that he was finished and ready to get up, he would just fuss and yell. Despite repeated attempts to teach him to use the signs for "more" and "all done," he kept communicating with his poor vocal skills instead. It was very hard to discern if he was being stubborn or was truly incapable. One morning after my husband complained about his constant fussing at the table and asked me to please teach him the signs, I decided it was training day. I was going to put some major effort into teaching this child to "use his signs and not his screams." So the stand-off began. I knew enough by this time to not start something like this if you weren't willing to persevere until the job was done. But I had no idea this time what I was getting myself into. I was soon to find out that I had given birth to one of the most strong-willed, persevering humans on earth. I had prayed that this child, Jeremiah, would be one who would be able to stand strong in the face of opposition just as the prophet Jeremiah in the Bible had. Now I was about to see the fruit of my prayers.

I made it clear to my baby that he needed to show me "more" or "all done" with his hands, and not only showed him over and over how to do it, but also helped him move his hands to do the motions. He fought me the whole way. But I told him he needed to not yell and to instead show mommy "more" or "all done," and that I wasn't getting him up until he did. After fifteen or twenty minutes of this, and him refusing to do it, I was feeling a major need for some wisdom from above. I went into the living room and began praying. I felt half crazy and like I had made a horrible choice in starting this stand off with my infant. But as I began to pray and ask God for wisdom in what to do, He began to show me that Jesus was a man of great authority but who walked in meekness because He was in submission to His heavenly Father. God was showing me that my Jeremiah needed to learn the same thing in order to use His persevering nature for the glory of God. It was important for me to teach this child that he could not be the one in charge. And God gave me peace that my baby was in fact capable of doing these signs and was just incredibly resistant to using them. So after a ridiculously long time (around three hours I think), and me kindly and calmly standing in front of him over and over (once about every five to ten minutes or so) showing him the signs and asking him to show me he was "all done," he finally did! It took a lot of prayer and wisdom to reach that victory though! I felt like I was in intense intercession for him, and if I hadn't sought God's wisdom in that situation, I would have never made it. I am very happy to report that after that "training day" he began using his signs and not his screams most of the time at the table. He still didn't really like using signs, but it certainly made for much more pleasant family dinners! And most importantly, a more peaceful and submissive child!

There are so many moments like these in a mom's life. We just aren't sure what to do and how to proceed with the challenges that face us! Whether it is what school to send them to (or not), how to handle a fight between siblings, how to deal with a character issue that keeps coming up, or any myriad of other things, we desperately need wisdom as mothers. The wonderful thing is that God has so graciously given us a promise in His Word, "But if any of you lacks wisdom, let him ask of God, who gives to all generously and without reproach, and it will be given him" (James 1:5). Wow! What a gift! He invites us, even implores us, to ask Him for wisdom! And He generously and freely gives it out to those who ask it of Him. We would be so foolish to not take Him up on this offer!

I can only imagine how important accessing this gift becomes as our children get older. For young ones, we need wisdom for how to train them, structure their day, and discipline them. But as they get older, new complications arise. They are trying to discover who they are and assert some independence, yet aren't quite mature enough to go without our voice and protection in their lives. Our need for wisdom on how to love them through this huge transitionary time is tremendous.

As our children grow, new challenges arise. I have found it is often difficult to know how to best handle some of the attitudes and actions my children are displaying. But I know I am the daughter of a very wise Father, and that He has invited me to come and ask Him for wisdom. When our daughter Hope developed a bad habit of lying (quite a lot in fact), God gave us wisdom to speak identity over her and to begin calling her Honest Hope. As my husband did this, it actually quickly broke her of the habit. There was something about speaking out a different identity over her that helped her to walk in that reality.

I have become increasingly thankful that God continuously puts me in challenging situations with my children where I need to depend on Him and His wisdom so desperately. And I am so very grateful that His answers are so wise!

God,
Thank You that You are the God of all wisdom, and that
You have invited us to ask You for wisdom. We do ask You
even now for greater wisdom in our mothering. Make us
wise mothers and help us to continuously tap into Your
wisdom as we go about our days.
Amen.

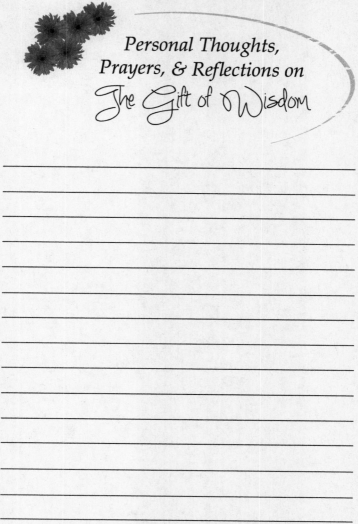

Personal Thoughts,
Prayers, & Reflections on
The Gift of Wisdom

_____
_____
_____
_____
_____
_____
_____
_____
_____
_____
_____
_____
_____

"For the Lord gives wisdom; from His mouth
come knowledge and understanding. He stores
up sound wisdom for the upright; He is a
shield to those who walk in integrity."

Proverbs 2:6-7

Chapter 17

THE GIFT OF REVELATION

Though closely connected to wisdom, I want to share a brief word on revelation. We serve a God who is a revealer of truth. Ephesians 1:17 says, " . . . that the God of our Lord Jesus Christ, the Father of glory, may give to you a spirit of wisdom and revelation in the knowledge of Him."

Revelation has an aspect of bringing truth and light to a person. We know that those who are not in Christ are in darkness, but as we come to Jesus, He begins to reveal truth to us and illuminate the reality of who Jesus is and the things of the Kingdom. However, we are on a journey and revelation is usually a process, not a one-time event.

Motherhood, for me, has been a conduit through which God has brought greater revelation to me of both who He is, as well as truths of His Kingdom. For example, after our third child was born, God took me on a journey of bringing me into a deeper revelation of how He sees children and the desire He has to bless parents with them. Through a number of ways, He began to get my attention and challenge me to surrender to Him my fertility. He opened my eyes to the many ways our culture has tainted our views on having children as well as the "ideal" number to have.

I began to see things from a new perspective, one that I believe was much more heavenly. I realized that most people decide when to have children based on emotions and/or practicality. They FEEL like it is a good time to have children, or that it is something they WANT in a particular time of life. Right before I found out that I was pregnant with Jeremiah, my third child, I had started to think that I didn't really want to be pregnant again for a little bit. I was starting to enjoy having my little ones sleep through the night and transitioning out of the infant stage. Then I found out I was pregnant. Sigh, laugh, surrender. But it wasn't until a little bit after he was born and I was being so blessed by what a gift he was that I began to realize that he was the child God knew I needed and gave me at the perfect time . . . but it was not what I thought I wanted and would not have chosen myself. I began to realize my emotions and fleeting circumstances were not a good way to decide when to have children. He also was releasing such a powerful revelation on what amazing gifts children are, that I began to think long and hard about limiting the number of gifts He might want to give me.

When this revelation settled in my heart, I knew He was asking my husband and I to fully surrender this area of our lives to Him. I have some amazing testimonies of what happened after this, and He has been so faithful to give us two more wonderful gifts since then in His perfect timing (with larger spaces in between the two as well!). I have experienced such peace in this surrender and am so incredibly thankful that God has given me this revelation in my personal journey of motherhood with Him.

There are so many deep revelations God wants to give to us. It has been so amazing to grow in a greater revelation of who God is as I have become a mother. Though it is a bit cliché, it is so true that as we experience such a deep love for our children, we gain a much greater understanding of how God sees us as His children. It is incredible to experience the unconditional love for our children we have as parents, and to realize that God has that same love, on a more perfect level, for us! As I observe my children and delight in them, I have learned that God delights in me in the same way. I have also learned some of why God desires my obedience so much as I realized that when my children listen to me it allows me to protect them and care for them better.

There are countless other revelations God brings us in motherhood: The revelation of how brief our time here on earth is as we watch our children grow from tiny newborn babes to young adults who then leave our home and are off on their own. The revelation of the Father's heart and how it breaks when one of His children rebels against Him, or how it bursts with joy when they walk in obedience. The revelation that our children ultimately belong to Him, and that as their Creator and Heavenly Father, His care for them is much deeper and greater than ours can ever be. May we embrace each revelation God wants to bring to us as moms, and let them forever change us, bringing us into more of the truth and light of the Kingdom of God.

God,
It is such a gift to be able to know You in a deeper way
by becoming a mom. Thank You for the deep revelations
that You give us as we parent our children. Help us to pay
attention to them and to come to know You as You reveal
Yourself and Your truth to us.
Amen.

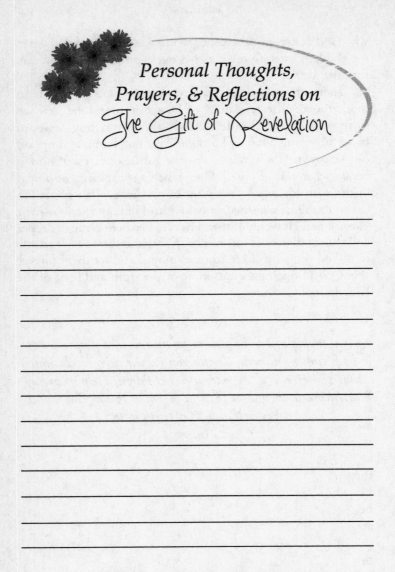

*Personal Thoughts,
Prayers, & Reflections on*
The Gift of Revelation

_____

_____

_____

_____

_____

_____

_____

_____

_____

_____

_____

_____

_____

_____

_____

_____

"... that the God of our Lord Jesus Christ, the
Father of glory, may give to you a spirit of wisdom
and of revelation in the knowledge of Him."

Ephesians 1:17

Chapter 18

THE GIFT OF SOWING

I have already referred to the garden analogy in a previous chapter, but I want to describe it further, as it is a wonderful word picture that parallels motherhood. God has so graciously allowed us the gift to be the predominate gardeners in our children's lives. As we plant seeds in them, we play a huge part in what will grow.

The gardener has the privilege of choosing what seeds he wants to plant. If he wants to grow flowers, he plants flower seeds; lettuce, he plants lettuce seeds; watermelon, watermelon seeds; and so on and so forth. A good gardener plants a variety of seeds, all things that are either tasty to eat or beautiful to look at. And then they have the gift of tending to them, watching those plants grow, and one day reaping a harvest from them. Like gardeners, we mothers are given a tremendous privilege of being able to sow into our children a variety of virtues, lessons, and skills.

As I watched one of my children sweep the kitchen floor this morning, I was blessed to think of how I am teaching her both the value and the skill of work. Through much labor and discipline on my part today (because she wasn't exactly sweeping willingly and joyfully yet), I am sowing seeds of discipline and hard work into my daughter that will one day sprout forth a strong work ethic.

I also love to sow into my children the truths and values of the Kingdom. We have the privilege of sowing righteousness, kindness, and love into their hearts, believing that God will indeed be faithful to produce a harvest of those things in their lives one day. Many of these "Kingdom seeds" are sown into our children by them watching, learning from, and imitating us. While sometimes this can be a little intimidating, it also makes me excited to think that I am modeling to them a life of faith and sowing into them a living example of how one lives a life for Jesus.

They watch and learn as we respond to death and tragedy by finding comfort in Jesus and putting our hope in Him. They get to see God's faithfulness as we trust Him for our financial needs and He provides with shining colors. They learn how to respond to conflict as we show them how to say sorry and forgive. They learn how to deal with their own sin as we model repentance to them in *our* lives. And they learn how to pray as we pray with and over them. These are seeds that are being planted firmly into their lives, and I believe with all my heart they will sprout forth one day into a beautiful harvest in each of my children.

What a blessing it will be to watch our children grow up to be godly men and women who know how to love well, serve well, work hard, and take the Kingdom with them wherever they go.

God,
Thank You for the honor and privilege it is to be
entrusted with the gift of sowing seeds into my children's
lives. I look forward in hope to the day when the harvest
of these seeds comes. Help me to be a wise and diligent
gardener and to choose Kingdom seeds of righteousness to
plant in their hearts. Help me to water and weed and
to trust You with the growth.
Amen.

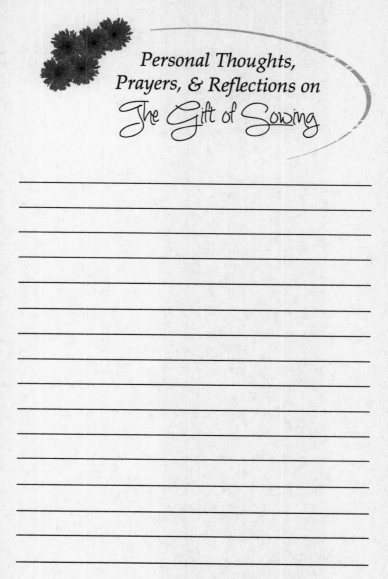

Personal Thoughts,
Prayers, & Reflections on
The Gift of Sowing

_____

_____

_____

_____

_____

_____

_____

_____

_____

_____

_____

_____

_____

_____

_____

_____

"Let us not lose heart in doing good, for in due
time we will reap if we do not grow weary."

Galatians 6:9

Chapter 19

THE GIFT OF WEAKNESS

The apostle Paul knew the gift of weakness by revelation from God. He penned the truth "for when I am weak, then I am strong" (2 Cor. 12:10) and found His strength in God alone. There is a gift that is available to us as believers that only comes through recognizing our weakness and inability. When we reach this place, we are able to begin leaning heavily on His strength and nothing else. We need to be able to recognize that His strength is infinitely stronger than any strength we can ever muster up on our own. 1 Corinthians 1:25 says that even the weakness of God is stronger than men.

So when I feel as though I have nothing left to give, or like I am not sure if I can make it another hour (much less another day), I am positioned in a perfect place to receive supernatural strength from God. I am able to recognize and realize how insufficient my own strength and abilities are, and I am forced to stop trying and start relying. This is how I should have been living all along, but so often it takes more intense circumstances to really bring us to our knees and force us into a place of weakness.

Herein lies the great gift that motherhood brings us. Perhaps you are somehow a mother who finds this job easy and are able to hold it all together. I, however, am most definitely not. Truth be told, I have never experienced anything harder in my whole life. Don't get me wrong, it is by far the best and most rewarding thing I have probably ever experienced. It is what I was made for, and it is also very fulfilling. But none of those truths take away the fact that it is also very challenging, and I often feel as though I am teetering on the brink of disaster. It seems like I have gotten myself in over my head and could drown at any minute. Enter weakness. But I am not left to my own devices and stuck in this place of drowning and helplessness. I am instead given the grace that comes only in a place of weakness: the grace of God lifting me up and placing me on the solid rock of Jesus from which I can never sink.

If anyone looks at my life and wonders how I do it all, the answer is by God's grace. But I believe the *key* is that I have learned one of the secrets of experiencing an abundance of God's grace—embracing weakness. Some people may think I am just a very strong, organized, capable person, and that is why I can have five kids, homeschool, do the ministry we do, etc. Nothing could be farther from the truth. Any strength I have completely comes from God, as I embrace *my* weakness and inability, and in turn receive *His* strength.

Let me share a personal example of embracing my weakness and experiencing God's strength in exchange. Recently, after my fifth child was born and I was trying to juggle a newborn, a child that needed an extra amount of help overcoming his dyslexia, a house with people in and out all day (the nature of our college-student ministry), a three-year old fighting for her way all the time, a seven-year-old who wants to rule the world, and a five-year-old who just doesn't like to listen E-V-E-R, I was definitely struggling to keep my head above water. There were days when I wanted to just shut myself in my room and not come out. But as I embraced my weakness and admitted I couldn't do it on my own, God began to flood in with His strength. His supernatural peace took over, and I was able to hold His hand and take things one task at a time (usually I would just stand at the sink and start to wash dishes). His grace was truly sufficient for me. But I have found that the secret is in embracing my weakness. Trying to pull myself up by my own bootstraps and prove that I am strong and can do it all only leaves me stressed out and failing.

So on those days where we feel like we have nothing left to give and all we can do is just try to survive, recognize the gift God is giving you in coming to Him and admitting your need and your weakness. Then receive the provision He has ready and waiting . . . the gift of His strength which is made perfect and complete in our weakness. It is a strength that never fails.

God,
Thank You that in my weakness You are made strong
and that Your grace is truly sufficient for me. Help me
to embrace weakness that I might tap into Your power.
I am so thankful for Your strength and that it
is available to me at all times.
Amen.

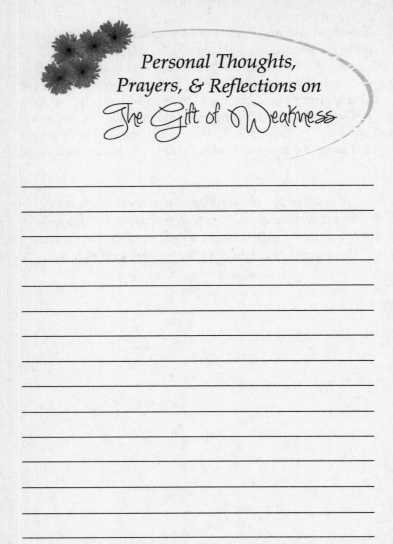

Personal Thoughts,
Prayers, & Reflections on
The Gift of Weakness

_____

_____

_____

_____

_____

_____

_____

_____

_____

_____

_____

_____

_____

_____

_____

"And He has said to me, 'My grace is sufficient for
you, for power is perfected in weakness.' Most gladly,
therefore, I will rather boast about my weaknesses,
so that the power of Christ may dwell in me."

(2 Corinthians 12:9)

Chapter 20

THE GIFT OF OVERCOMING

I am certain every mom on the face of the planet has had that feeling of being overwhelmed more than once. And for some of us, it has felt like an all-too-familiar friend. As I have already mentioned, the pressures on us as moms is so intense, so overwhelming, that sometimes it feels like we are sinking in quicksand with no help in sight.

Yet, we have a Helper, and He is committed to our victory. He has promised us that we will not drown, that we can walk though the fire and not be burned (Isaiah 43:2). This means that we will overcome. No matter what difficulties come our way, no matter how great our challenges, in Christ we can live as overcomers. A victorious life is our inheritance.

God has given His children an abundance of promises in regards to overcoming our afflictions and challenges in life. Another one is found in 2 Corinthians 4:7-8,

> *"But we have this treasure in earthen vessels, so that the surpassing greatness of the power will be of God and not from ourselves; we are afflicted in every way, but not crushed; perplexed, but not despairing; persecuted, but not forsaken; struck down, but not destroyed . . . "*

God promises to not allow us to be destroyed or crushed under the weight of life. We need to have faith that He is willing and able to give us the power to overcome.

When I was in my most recent pregnancy, feeling rather overwhelmed with life and the four children I already had, compounded by some of the challenges of the pregnancy, it took a tremendous amount of faith to trust God to see me through all that was happening. A song kept playing on the radio that God gave me as a theme song for my season: "Overcomer" by Mandisa. The chorus says,

> "You're an overcomer. Stay in the fight 'til the final round. You're not going under, because God is holding you right now. You might be down for a moment, feeling like it's hopeless, that's when He reminds you, that you're an overcomer. You're an overcomer."

As I would drive around to the grocery store or to my prenatal appointments, He so graciously allowed this song to come on the radio over and over. I was continually reminded that this was my inheritance as His child. I was going to overcome and make it through this season, not by the skin of my teeth, but instead with flying colors.

Many of us have been through very challenging circumstances in life: the loss of a child, a parent, our home, sometimes even our sanity. It feels like we aren't going to make it; however, we can still overcome because of Jesus and what He has done for us.

> "For whatever is born of God overcomes the world; and this is the victory that has overcome the world—our faith. Who is the one who overcomes the world, but he who believes that Jesus is the Son of God?" (1 John 5:4-5).

The secret to overcoming is our faith—the very first gift I listed in the book. Our faith is simply trusting in God, trusting that He is true and that what He says is true. It is believing in

His promises and provision, and knowing that He is indeed faithful to give us the victory. It is believing that we will overcome, not because of what we do or our own strength, but because we belong to Him. It is a promise to all who believe and will receive this gift from His hands.

God,
Words cannot express how thankful I am for Your promise
that I can be an overcomer. Thank You for providing for our
victory as believers. Give me the faith necessary to overcome
the many trials that come my way in life and to receive
Your power to live victoriously.
Amen.

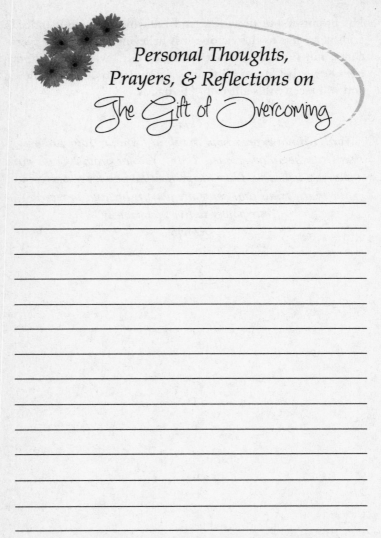

Personal Thoughts,
Prayers, & Reflections on
The Gift of Overcoming

_____

_____

_____

_____

_____

_____

_____

_____

_____

_____

_____

_____

_____

_____

_____

"When you pass through the waters, I will be with
you; and through the rivers, they will not overflow
you. When you walk through the fire, you will
not be scorched, nor will the flame burn you."

Isaiah 43:2

Chapter 21

THE GIFT OF COMMUNITY

It seems a common complaint in motherhood is that we can't ever seem to get any alone time. We often can't even go to the bathroom by ourselves! And while I admit it can feel a bit overwhelming at times, I would like to propose that we flip the way we see this. In many ways we live in a very isolated culture, and so many people are lonely. Now granted, a nine-month-old isn't necessarily the most stimulating company, but it doesn't mean that God isn't giving us a gift by allowing us people with whom to live our moment by moment lives with. Having children means we often don't have to be alone anymore.

Not only that, but we get the gift of being able to develop real and true relationships with some of the people we love and care about more than anyone else—our children. So much of scripture speaks about relationships. Yet how can we experience these realities and this significant aspect of the Kingdom of God without engaging in real and lasting relationships? And what better place to do that than in our relationships with our children?

As I was driving our huge, 12-passenger van today, with my kids all buckled into their car seats, I realized that instead of seeing my children as little people that I have to always take with me everywhere I go, God wants me to see the gift of the community He is developing within our family. On one hand, having five little kids makes it feel so hard to leave the house and just go run a basic errand. On the other hand, when we all got into the car today to make a "quick" trip (I can guarantee you nothing is ever quick with this circus) to grab some basic items at the store, we were able to fellowship with one another and enjoy each other's company. In our families we have the opportunity to know each other so well, and if we will be willing to engage in it, we can learn how to be each other's greatest sources of encouragement, forgiveness, compassion, and unconditional love.

Instead of living lonely, isolated lives, God wants to develop a Kingdom community right where we are as mothers . . . within our own home. Our children are such an integral part of the community that He is building. Though five children might sound like a lot to some people, I can honestly say that when one is gone somewhere, we can really feel their presence missing. It almost seems lonely, and certainly out of balance. I can literally feel the incompleteness of our family. However, when we are all together, there is a rightness to it; that strong sense of community and unity of our whole family being together. What a tremendous blessing!

God,
Thank You for the amazing gift of community You have
provided me by giving me children to live life with.
May we embrace this gift and learn to dwell together
in a loving, encouraging, peaceful way.
Amen.

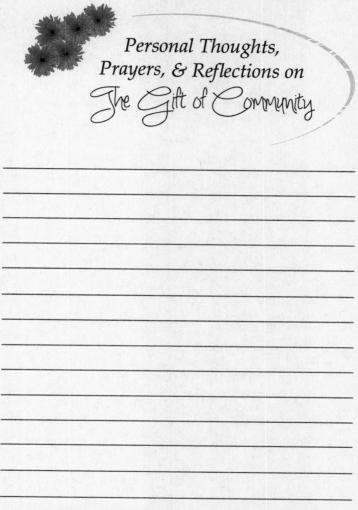

Personal Thoughts, Prayers, & Reflections on
The Gift of Community

_____

_____

_____

_____

_____

_____

_____

_____

_____

_____

_____

_____

_____

_____

"Behold, how good and how pleasant it is for brothers to
dwell together in unity! It is like the precious oil upon the
head, coming down upon the beard . . . it is like the dew
of Hermon coming down upon the mountains of Zion;
for there the Lord commanded the blessing—life forever."

Psalm 133:1, 3

Chapter 22

THE GIFT OF LETTING GO

Ilove how God has used motherhood to help me learn to let go and trust Him more. I believe it is common to want to be in control, and certainly to want things to run smoothly and effectively. But that is just not the reality of this life on earth. Rarely do things go the way we want.

Children have a natural built-in gift to help adults—especially their parents—learn how to let go of their expectations, their selfishness, and their desire for things to be easy, clean, simple, or fast. There are so many ways that children challenge us to relax, slow down, and let go of our own agendas and plans. I think it is one of the things that makes kids so amazing. They (usually) haven't yet taken on the pressures of this world: the pressure to be productive, to perform, or to have everything be perfect. They know how to enjoy life!

My husband loves to use the analogy of living life "white-knuckled," as opposed to "open-handed." When we are holding onto things tightly, our hands aren't very available to reach out and receive the many gifts God is wanting to give us. He wants us to surrender our dreams, entitlements, expectations, and strivings into His hands and trust that He is faithful and He is enough. As we know, He doesn't always give us all we want, but He truly is faithful to give us what we need if we will be open to receive it and will lay down our desire to be in control.

I think letting go and surrendering comes easier for some than others. Some moms really want to hold a tight grip on things. I have found that this is commonly due to fear. Being able to let go of things—whether it is our frustration at the house being a mess, or the fact that our lives just aren't all we had hoped they would be at this point—comes from a deeper trust in Jesus. He gives us the opportunity in motherhood to learn how to let go and grow in our trust of Him, knowing that life is about more than just having our day run smoothly.

The reality of letting go of our dreams, hopes, and expectations does not mean we cannot have a plan and a vision for our lives. It just means that we need to trust God more than our plan and be okay with things not going how we want. When will we realize that our lives as moms rarely go according to plan?! It's twenty minutes past my three-year-old's bed time, so I "plan" to do an extra quick bedtime routine. But she insists that she put her own pajamas on (at a speed that makes a ninety-year-old look fast), doesn't cooperate with brushing her teeth (why did I think she would when she never does), and then decides she needs to go poop before bed tonight. Instead of a quick bedtime routine, this just broke the record for the slowest one. So when those moments come where *my* plan is anything but the reality, or those moments of chaos and unpredictability unfold, am I going to try to frustratingly control everything? Or will I choose to stay in peace and simply let go?

I find that often it is in the small things that I am tested the most in my ability to let go and trust God. For example, I wanted to get four specific things accomplished this morning, but have only gotten two done because of a scraped knee, two poopy bottoms to wipe, and a conversation I had to have with the child that decided to shove his sister down then step on her. Nothing is going according to my plan! Of course, over the years I have learned that if I want to plan out my day, I better factor in time for all of these things, because this is the reality of life right now. But at the heart of it is the reality that I need to let go and let Jesus be in charge. Then I will be able to find the true peace, strength, and provision I am so desperately in need of. And I praise Him that He is better at managing my life than I am.

Finally, letting go is key to living a life filled with the Spirit. If we are trying to be the ones in control, we are not yielded to the Holy Spirit. I long to live in a way where I am controlled by the Holy Spirit, not by my own agenda, fears, worries, striving, or well-laid plans.

This is all part of the beauty of living the exchanged life . . . my life for His, my worries for His care, my lack for His bounty, my fear for His peace. As moms we need to realize it is not our job to try to manage our stress and anxiety. Instead it is our job to lay it down and let God care for us. As we let go, He will be given room to be exalted in our lives and show forth His amazing faithfulness!

God,
Help me to learn to let go. I don't want to strive anymore
and to try so hard to manage my own life. Help me
to open up my hands to You and to surrender everything
into YOUR very capable hands. Thank You that You
are powerful and faithful and can manage everything
perfectly. I will rest in You.
Amen.

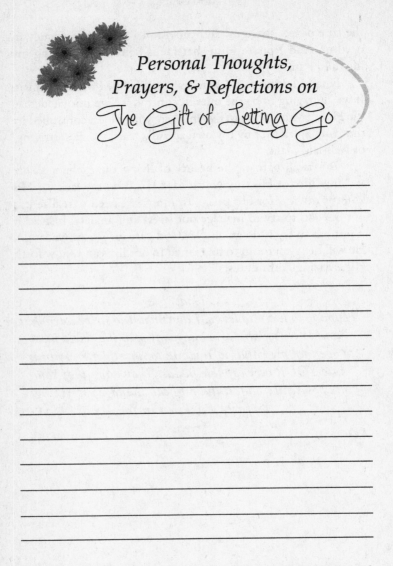

Personal Thoughts, Prayers, & Reflections on
The Gift of Letting Go

_____

_____

_____

_____

_____

_____

_____

_____

_____

_____

_____

_____

"Therefore humble yourselves under the mighty hand of God, that He may exalt you at the proper time, casting all your anxiety on Him, because He cares for you."

1 Peter 5:7

Chapter 23

THE GIFT OF SHAPING LIVES

I believe God has called us to all be artists. It doesn't mean we will all paint or sculpt, but as children of the ultimate Artist, I do believe part of being created in the image of God, our Creator, is that He has placed within us a desire and need to create. One person's art may be a garden, another's may be their home interior. Some are called to create art in their business, while others are called to create art via their music, engineering designs, or inventions. No matter what the medium is, to create is to partake in the nature of the Divine.

As mothers, I believe our art and the medium with which we create are the hearts and lives of our children. What an honor and privilege it is to be called to shape lives! May we never neglect or take lightly the awesome and powerful gift God has given us as moms.

No other person has the power to shape the lives of my children as significantly as I do. Obviously, fathers play a very powerful role in this as well, but moms seem to have an even more influential position in this as the primary care-giver and nurturer.

I often see my role as a mother in the metaphor of the potter. I do not believe that my children are born as lumps of clay waiting for me to mold and shape them according to my choosing, because God is the true potter. Instead, I believe that they are already created as unique vessels from God, and it is my job to partake in the shaping *with* God, who already knows who they were born to be. Therefore, it is important that as I do my shaping and molding work, I understand God's heart and design for these creations of His.

Perhaps He has created one of my children to be a pitcher and another a bowl. I have the honor of helping shape that pitcher to be tall, sturdy, and pour well, and the bowl to be strong, wide, and deep. I can also help create intricate and beautiful designs on the outsides. I believe God allows us to co-create with Him, even in our children's lives.

So how do I want to shape my children? For me, I want to etch gratitude onto their hearts and shape them with kindness so that it may be an attribute they walk out in their own lives. I want to model freedom, honor, and a deep love for those around us. I want to help shape them into radical lovers of Jesus who know how to live by faith. The ways I am called to shape my children are not going to be exactly the same for another mom. But as I intentionally participate in this work, I am given the amazing privilege of shaping these little lives. I cannot help but see the wonderful gift this is to us as moms; one we must take seriously and steward well.

God,
You are the potter and we are the clay. Thank You that You have created me and my children, and You are shaping and molding us according to Your plan. Help me to engage in the process of molding my children in the ways You desire. Thank You for the privilege it is to be a tool in Your hands to help shape them with You.
Amen.

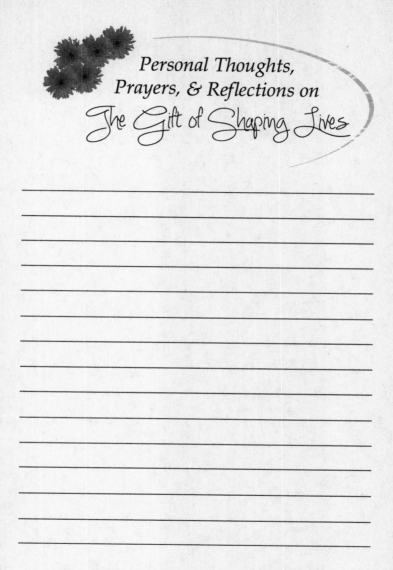

Personal Thoughts,
Prayers, & Reflections on

The Gift of Shaping Lives

_____

_____

_____

_____

_____

_____

_____

_____

_____

_____

_____

_____

_____

_____

"But now, O Lord, You are our Father, we
are the clay, and You our potter; and all
of us are the work of Your hand."

Isaiah 64:8

THE GIFT OF EXPONENTIAL INFLUENCE

One thing I really love about being a mom is the fact that I now roll with a whole posse of world changers. I have always wanted to change the world, but I used to feel very limited in my influence. Whether I lacked the boldness, time, or reach, I never seemed to be able to influence as many people as I desired.

Now that I am getting to so profoundly influence and train up my children, each of whom are so unique with their own strengths and weaknesses, I can already see how much more powerful we are together than separate. There is just something about a whole brood that makes people have to stop and listen. Even if we aren't using words, our lives speak louder because of the power of numbers.

Not only are we "louder" because of the power of our numbers, I am also able to reach so many more people because of the extended reach my children now have. Though they are still fairly young, they already touch hearts in a way I never could. Even their faith extends out onto others without them even trying. We had a girl in our church come to know Jesus because she was drawn in by wanting to babysit our children. Then one time a guy in the church who was struggling with anxiety and worry was profoundly ministered to by my oldest son (who was about six at the time) because he said a simple comment to the guy along the lines of, "God is with you and it will be okay." My daughter Hope, who is currently seven, and our resident evangelist, often asks random strangers if they know God. And as our children get older and we continue to pour more and more into their hearts and minds, their impact will be so much greater on this world than we ever could have had alone.

A picture I love that represents this idea comes from a favorite verse of mine in Psalm 127:3-4, "Behold, children are a gift of the Lord, the fruit of the womb is a reward. Like arrows in the hand of a warrior, so are the children of one's youth." If these children we are raising are being likened to arrows in our hand, this means that we can one day put them into our bow and shoot them out into the earth to carry God's Kingdom with them and change the world. They are powerful and will have a far-reaching influence, as well as be used to knock down the enemy, as we love them and sharpen them each day.

So for those of us out there like me who have always wanted to change the world for Christ, and have perhaps felt as though having children has somehow taken us away from that call, just know that the truth is our influence is only compounding and growing because of our children. What an awesome gift!

God,
Thank You that You understand exponential growth and
influence. You desire that Your people multiply and grow in
their impact on this earth. I am so thankful that You
have allowed me to do this by having children and pouring
into them my all so that they might go into the earth
and bring great influence. Guide me as I do this,
and let our family bring You great glory.
Amen.

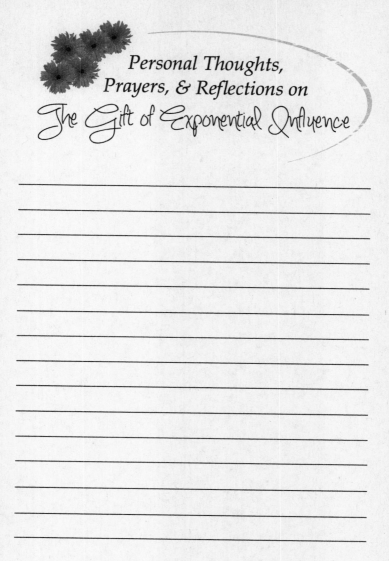

Personal Thoughts,
Prayers, & Reflections on

The Gift of Exponential Influence

"The things which you have heard from me in the
presence of many witnesses, entrust these to faithful
men who will be able to teach others also."

2 Timothy 2:2

Chapter 25

THE GIFT OF FREEDOM FROM SELF

One night I was sitting in a home group setting with young people from our church. The room was filled with mostly college students, and a discussion arose about the struggles many of them had when coming into social settings. Insecurities would arise for most of them, and they would respond by withdrawing and being overly concerned about how others perceived them.

As I listened to these honest, common, and understandable struggles, I discovered yet another gift God has given me in motherhood. Though at one time I could have identified with these insecurities and social challenges, I realized it was a far-off and faint memory for me. Then it hit me . . . I hadn't had the time to feel that way in years. Having children had set me free from being so concerned about myself!

Being constantly trained to think about others by my young and needy children, I had unknowingly learned how to stop worrying so much about myself and how *I* was feeling, how *I* was doing, and what other people were thinking about *me.* God had set me free! He had given me an incredible gift via motherhood to learn how to truly put others first. He had trained me in how to be about others, not in a self-demeaning way, but rather in a freeing way. I have had to learn how to put my security and identity solely in Him and in the process have become free to not have to worry about myself and my needs so much. There just simply wasn't time for that anymore.

It wasn't that I had written myself off or believed that I wasn't important. It was just that God had taught me how to look to Him to fill my needs instead of others, and this freed me to love out of a pure, selfless heart. Our children are not intended to meet our needs and that actually empowers us to stop living selfishly, focus on others, and be set free from ourselves! God had secretly taught me how to live out Philippians 2:3-7, which says,

> *"Do nothing from selfishness or empty conceit, but with humility of mind regard one another as more important than yourselves; do not merely look out for your own personal interests, but also for the interests of others."*

There are days when even being able to go to the bathroom gets pushed aside for several hours as I am busy meeting the needs of my children. Putting them first and making sure they are even fed and clothed each day, much less caring for their hearts and minds, does not leave a lot of time and energy to dwell excessively on *my* needs and desires. I am not claiming to have this down perfectly by any means, and selfishness certainly creeps in from time to time. But the fact that my focus is usually not on myself has brought a lot of freedom and healing over the years. What an incredible gift for the child of God—to go from insecurity and selfishness to loving freely from a pure heart!

God,
Thank You for setting me free from self. The burden of living selfishly and overly concerned about myself is too heavy. Thank You for giving me children who help pull my eyes off of myself and teach me how to put others first. I am so thankful that You want to teach me daily how to lay down my life for others and in the process find true freedom.
Amen.

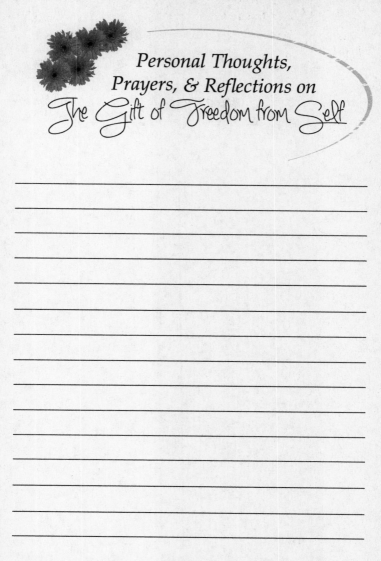

Personal Thoughts,
Prayers, & Reflections on
The Gift of Freedom from Self

"We know love by this, that He laid down His life for us;
and we ought to lay down our lives for the brethren."

1 John 3:16

Chapter 26

THE GIFT OF RIGHTEOUSNESS

One of the first gifts God gives to the new believer is the gift of righteousness. Many scriptures speak to this reality; particularly the book of Romans is full of the truth about our righteousness in Christ. We even see it in God's prototype of Abraham, who was credited righteousness not by what he did, but because he believed what God said to him.

In the New Covenant, God imparts the righteousness of Jesus to the believer. Romans 4:5 says, "But to the one who does not work, but believes in Him who justifies the ungodly, his faith is credited as righteousness," and 2 Corinthians 5:21 says, "He made Him who knew no sin to be sin on our behalf, so that we might become the righteousness of God in Him."

Scripture makes it very clear that our righteousness has nothing to do with our actions, our behavior, or our personality. It has everything to do with who Jesus is and the perfect life that He lived. Because of our faith in Him, the righteousness of Christ is imparted to us . . . given freely as a gift.

It seems feelings of guilt and failure are very familiar to most moms. We so often condemn ourselves for not being perfect. Whether we feel guilty that we didn't do or give enough, or shameful after speaking too harshly or acting too impatiently, there are many opportunities for the enemy to come in and condemn us.

We must realize that we are not perfect, but God is not surprised by that. That is why Jesus came. He came to live the perfect life that we could not live and then to impart to us His righteousness. When our conscience tries to condemn us, the Bible tells us that God is greater than our hearts (1 John 3:20), and we have been given a promise that "therefore there is now no condemnation for those who are in Christ Jesus" (Romans 8:1).

So when we have messed up (a common occurrence in my experience of motherhood), we need to resist the temptation to wallow in our shame and condemnation (i.e., take ourselves out of the game and put ourselves into the penalty box). The accuser of the brethren (Rev. 12:10) will try to condemn us and keep us in guilt. But we must know that we have been given an incredible gift of righteousness through Jesus.

As mothers, we need to remember that we can come to God confidently and with assurance, despite our shortcomings and failings, because of the blood of Jesus that cleanses us of our sin. Hebrews 10:19-22 explains this reality for us,

> "Therefore, brethren, since we have confidence to enter the holy place by the blood of Jesus, by a new and living way which He inaugurated for us through the veil, that is, His flesh, and since we have a great priest over the house of God, let us draw near with a sincere heart in full assurance of faith, having our hearts sprinkled clean from an evil conscience and our bodies washed with pure water."

I am thankful to say that there have been many times that God has ministered this truth to me after I have "blown it" with my children. I wish I could say that I am always calm and loving with my kids, but that would be a lie. There are so many situations where my children get the best of me and anger and frustration are my response. I am often left feeling guilty and condemned afterwards, and it is a painful feeling. But as I have learned to not only humble myself before them and apologize, but to also quickly repent before God, I am learning to receive His forgiveness and grace more fully. I realize my inheritance is a clean conscience, and that despite my sin and shortcomings, He still sees me as righteous and clean. It is a truly amazing gift and one we must continually open as moms!

God,
Words cannot express how thankful I am for the gift of
righteousness. You know that I am far from perfect and still
fall short every day. Thank You for Your one time sacrifice
that has made me clean for all time. Thank You for offering
continuous forgiveness and freedom from condemnation.
Help me to live in that reality every day.
Amen.

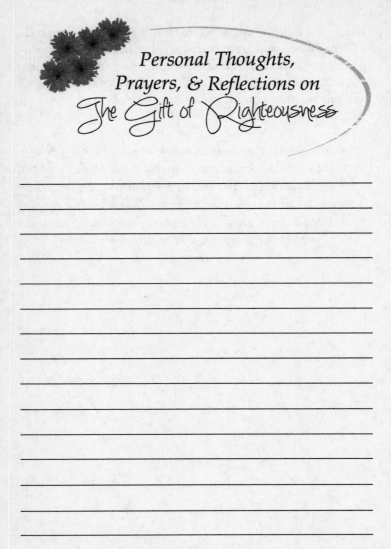

Personal Thoughts,
Prayers, & Reflections on
The Gift of Righteousness

_____

_____

_____

_____

_____

_____

_____

_____

_____

_____

_____

_____

_____

_____

_____

_____

_____

"For if by the transgression of the one, death reigned
through the one, much more those who receive the
abundance of grace and the gift of righteousness
will reign in life through the One, Jesus Christ."

Romans 5:17

Chapter 27

THE GIFT OF TRUE IDENTITY

I am a good mom. While I don't necessarily always *act* like a good mom should, I am still a good mom. At one point I started to struggle with identifying myself as an angry mom. At another time, it was that I was a disorganized mom. Or a lazy mom. But then God started showing me that identifying myself in these ways was neither helpful nor true.

I have come to learn that we will live out, or manifest, that which we believe. If we believe that we are sinners condemned to forever struggle with our weaknesses, we will stay stuck in that place and never grow out of it. Yet, if we believe what God says about who we are and what He wants to accomplish in and through us, we will be unstoppable.

In my struggles with sin, I need to look at who *He* says I am, and what kind of mom *He* made me to be. Then I need to allow Him to empower me to live that out.

Because of the gift of righteousness that comes from Christ (see previous chapter), I am now a new creation (2 Cor. 5:17) and have been set free from the power of sin and death (Rom. 8:2). Even though it doesn't mean I never sin, it does mean that I am not a *slave* to sin anymore (Romans 6:6-7) and that my identity is no longer a sinner, but a saint. I have been set free from sin and empowered by grace to live rightly, just as

Romans 6:18 declares, "and having been freed from sin, you became slaves of righteousness."

If you look up the use of the terms "sinner" and "saint" in the Bible, you will see that the term "sinner" is applied to unbelievers, but that those who have put their faith in Christ are referred to repeatedly as "saints." We have been purified through the blood of Jesus, and our new true identity is that we are no longer sinners, but those who have been set free from the power of sin and are living as sanctified and set apart "holy ones" on the earth.

In my struggle with anger and impatience as a mom, God has shown me that the more I dwell on who I really am in Christ, the more my actions begin to line up with these truths. He reminds me that I am the righteousness of God in Christ Jesus (2 Cor. 5:21), and a beloved daughter of God (John 1:12). I have been cleansed and forgiven (1 Cor. 6:11 & Col. 2:13), and I have the Holy Spirit living in me (1 Cor. 6:19). As a result of this, the *fruit* of the Spirit is available to me, which means I am able to live full of love, joy, peace, patience, kindness, goodness, gentleness, and self-control (Gal. 5:22-23). This means the truth is that I am a gentle, kind, and loving mom. Now, sometimes I have a slight identity crisis and may stop *acting* like I am these things. This is when I am living out of my flesh. But my actions are never my true identity.

I have never met a Jesus-following mom who does not passionately do her best to love her family. Yet we are all so aware of our weaknesses and failings. I truly believe that the Father is speaking over us mothers that we are His beloved daughters and it is time we become more aware of how God sees us. He does not dwell on our weaknesses. He sees our hearts—the hearts that are desiring desperately to love Him and our children well. He sees us as new creations that are filled with the Holy Spirit and are growing into all that He created us to be.

We need to extend this same grace to our children as well. We must see them as who God created them to be, even when they are struggling to live this way. This enables us as their parents to call them into their true identity. Sometimes I will gently remind my daughters to remember to act like the princesses they are—they *are* daughters of a King after all. The example of calling our daughter Honest Hope when she was struggling with lying is a testimony of how speaking true identity over our children is so powerful. It really enables them to walk in who God has created and called them to be. May we all receive the gift of true identity, both for our children and ourselves as well.

God,
Thank You that You see me through eyes of grace. Thank You for setting me free from the power of sin. Thank You for the gift of Your Holy Spirit who dwells in me and brings forth the fruit of the Spirit in my life. Help me to see myself as You see me and empower me to live free from sin and as the saint you say I am.
Amen.

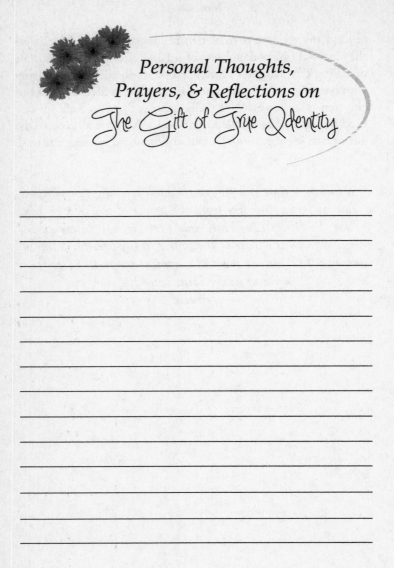

Personal Thoughts,
Prayers, & Reflections on
The Gift of True Identity

_____
_____
_____
_____
_____
_____
_____
_____
_____
_____
_____
_____
_____
_____
_____

"Therefore if anyone is in Christ, he is a
new creature; the old things have passed
away; behold, new things have come."

2 Corinthians 5:17

Chapter 28

THE GIFT OF OUR CHILDREN

The most obvious and greatest gift God gives us in motherhood is the gift of our children. Each one of our children is a gift straight from the hand of God, a gift bigger than just about anything we have ever been given on earth. Their names and faces should be the first things we think of when we think of the gifts God has given us in motherhood.

I have a number of friends who have either not been able to get pregnant at all or had a very hard time getting pregnant. If you are one of those moms, you are more aware than many of us of what a gift your child or children are. Sometimes after years of waiting and longing for a child, the hope of ever having one can feel so elusive and impossible. And then by some miracle, God brings you a child. Whether through adoption or conception, that child is a gift that you are dramatically aware of and exuberantly thankful for.

For those of us who have not had this struggle, it can be easier to take our children for granted. I'm sure even the mother who struggled to get pregnant still has moments of taking her child for granted. We tend to take for granted that which we always have available.

Yet we must do all that we can to take time to recognize the gifts God has given us in each individual child we get to mother. They are so precious in the sight of God, and He has given them to us as gifts to treasure and steward. They are lives that He has entrusted to us, to mold and shape and care for, to pray for and encourage, and to help bring into their destinies. This is one of the greatest privileges we can have on earth . . . to receive God's children and to be able to give them back to Him, trusting Him and HIS purposes for them.

So far I have been given five treasures, five amazing and astounding gifts in my children. Samuel is the serious, thoughtful child, the one who loves to follow all the rules and make sure others are too. He is going to change the world with his tender heart and his love for truth and righteousness. He is already a godly young man with a sensitive side and a deep knowledge of God and the Kingdom.

Hope is my firecracker, the one who may very well take over several companies and possibly nations. She already at age seven intimidates many adults as well as most children. She loves ferociously and is very in tune with the Holy Spirit, though she still needs to learn how to heed what He is wanting.

Jeremiah, the five-year-old, is our third gift, and was the child God brought me just when I needed him and didn't really know it or want it. He is the most tenacious and persevering person I have ever met. He is a bit ornery at times, but also can be so tender and loving. One of his nicknames is "Snug-Love" because he is our one child that actually likes to snuggle. He is going to be just like the prophet Jeremiah in the Bible, obeying God in spite of what everyone else thinks about it. That is the tenacity and perseverance we can already see.

Then there is our fourth little blessing, Joanna Joy. She is truly a joy and a delight, and one of the funniest people most of us know. She is our three-year-old vocal and joyful child, cute as a button, and wanting to assert her independence in everything.

Last, but certainly not least, is the baby, Isaac. It is always so nice to have a baby in the house. Everyone loves Isaac, and he really is the best baby I have ever had. He is such a happy, smiley, and sweet baby, and blesses me every day. I could write whole chapters on each of my children and the gifts they are. But what about you? What about your children? Are you recognizing the gifts they are instead of focusing on their challenges?

When I was able to see what a gift each child was, it wasn't so hard to realize that I should be open to as many gifts as He wanted to bring us. Personally, I love gifts, and could never imagine turning one down. So I realized I didn't want to turn any gifts down from God either. If He wanted to give us a child, who was I to reject that gift? We began a walk of even greater faith than we first thought having children would be, and it has brought greater joy and peace than I thought possible. So I am happy to report that Lord willing, one day my list of gifts (a.k.a. children) will be a little bit longer!

God,
Words cannot express how thankful I am that You have
blessed me with children. I am overwhelmed by Your
goodness and generosity. Forgive me for the many times
I take this gift for granted. Help me to enjoy my children and
to treasure them always as my greatest gift in motherhood.
Amen.

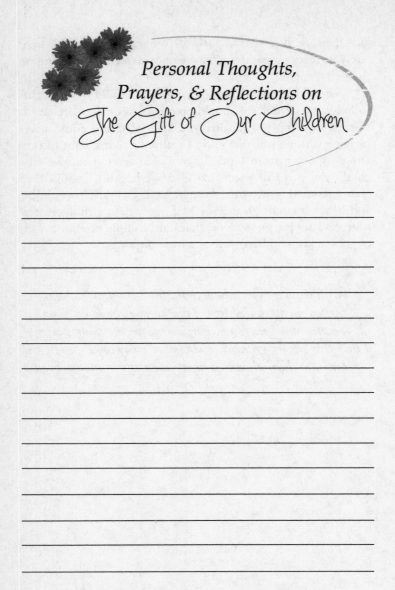

Personal Thoughts, Prayers, & Reflections on

The Gift of Our Children

_____

_____

_____

_____

_____

_____

_____

_____

_____

_____

_____

_____

_____

_____

_____

_____

_____

_____

"Behold, children are a gift of the Lord,
the fruit of the womb is a reward."

Psalm 127:3

Chapter 29

THE GIFT OF WHOLENESS

While there is much we lose in motherhood (sleep, time, elements of our freedom), there is so much more that we gain. Hopefully these many gifts I have written about are just a small sampling of that reality. One last gift that is worth pointing out is that through motherhood God desires to give us the gift of wholeness.

"But women will be saved through childbearing . . . " (1 Timothy 2:15 NIV). I still remember when I was eighteen and read this verse and was so perplexed by it that I asked one of the leaders of my missions team to explain it. Why I went to a twenty-five-year-old male to ask this question is a mystery to me! And his answer was pitiful. I moved on, and it took about six more years before someone was able to give me what I believe the true explanation of this verse is. It lies in the little Greek word "sozo," which means "to save, to rescue, to heal, to deliver, to make whole." "Soteria" is the word used for salvation in the New Testament, and the meaning of the word is "wholeness." It encapsulates a much fuller salvation than we are usually taught in our Sunday School lessons. It is not just a salvation from sin and hell. The real meaning of "sozo" and "soteria" is fullness of life. It is salvation that includes our healing, deliverance, and wholeness.

Having now been a mom for a decade, I can see God's gift

to me of bringing about a greater wholeness, healing, and salvation through motherhood. This verse has begun to make sense to me finally. A good translation of the verse could be, "But women will be *made whole* through childbearing . . . "

There was a part of me that was lacking something major before I was given my children. Not only was I lacking the capacity to truly live outside of my own selfishness and desires, I was also lacking the ability to love more fully and completely. My children have drawn out of me love that I never knew existed before. It is a self-sacrificial, unconditional, total and complete love. It is a love that helps us to understand the powerful and unconditional love the Father has for His children, and for us personally.

The many gifts I have written about in this book are all examples of how God uses having children to bring about sanctification and wholeness in our lives. I am so thankful for this gift. He has truly made us to be mothers, and while it is one of the hardest things we will ever do, it is also one of the most rewarding. Not only because we have the blessing of our children, but also because of the amazing things He does in our lives through the journey of raising them.

God,
Thank You for Your commitment to making me whole,
complete, and lacking in nothing. I am so thankful for the
many gifts You have given me in motherhood that have been
used to teach me, grow me, and bring wholeness in
my life. You are such a good Father and Your blessings
are so abundant in my life.
Amen.

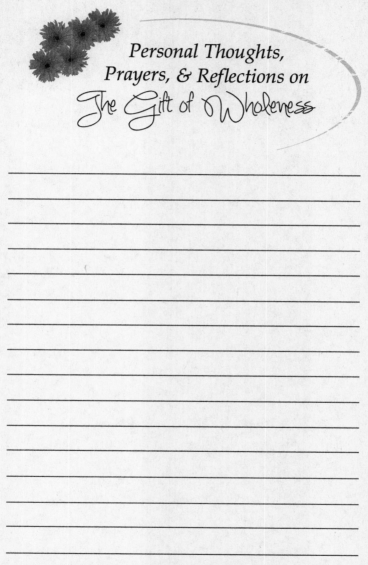

Personal Thoughts,
Prayers, & Reflections on
The Gift of Wholeness

_____

_____

_____

_____

_____

_____

_____

_____

_____

_____

_____

_____

_____

_____

_____

"And let endurance have its perfect result, so that you
may be perfect and complete, lacking in nothing."

James 1:4

ENDLESS GIFTS

Every mother could write her own book on the specific gifts God has given her in and through motherhood. The list could go on and on. I think the point is to learn a new way to view not only motherhood, but life.

As Ann Voskamp's *One Thousand Gifts* has so profoundly challenged me to realize, counting our gifts from God can do a miraculous work in our lives and hearts. It is a perspective issue. It is so easy to notice and point out what is going wrong in our lives. In fact, many of us dwell on it incessantly. It takes a supernatural outlook to instead take time to notice all of the grace that God is continually pouring out upon us. He is an extravagant God, showering us with an abundance of blessings, if only we will take time to notice. "And God is able to make all grace abound to you, so that always having all sufficiency in everything, you may have an abundance for every good deed" (2 Corinthians 9:8).

When one of my best friends, Becky Jo Cumming, came to visit with her husband and six little girls (age eight and under), God began opening my eyes to specific gifts and graces He had poured out on her and her family. I was amazed to see how *different* they were than what He had given me as a mom. I started to realize that because it was the only experience of motherhood she knew, she wasn't really able to notice these gifts most of the time. So I began to point them out to her as I would notice something specific and unique that God had blessed them with in their family or in her motherhood. First it was her ability to almost effortlessly keep up with nursing the baby, feeding the toddler, and giving all of the older girls snacks. Then it was the way the four-year-old was so drawn to the infant and was completely trustworthy and helpful with her. Many of these things were gifts I did *not* have going on in my motherhood experience. But I began to see that in the same way Becky Jo had not noticed many of these small little graces (that make a big difference in our day to day lives), I was most likely doing the same thing. Had I ever stopped to notice the grace God had given me by allowing my fourth born to LOVE laying on the trampoline while I jump on it, and God thereby giving me an opportunity to exercise? Or, as many other mom friends have pointed out to me, that God has graced me with a high tolerance for mess? Not that I enjoy it or ever have that as the goal, but if it occurs, it doesn't really affect me or stress me out too much. Those are both specific gifts in my journey, ones that are no doubt from God, and His provision for what I need along the way.

It was a powerful lesson for me to learn that God is blessing me with specific gifts and graces in our family and in my mothering, but I am often not aware and noticing them. This really challenged me to pay attention. As a believer, the gifts are always there because we have a good Father who desires to give good gifts to His children. Whether it is a beautiful sunset, a special moment with a child, or simply the fact that two of my five children play well together, the gifts are endless. It is simply a matter of allowing God to open our eyes to see from that perspective.

"If grace is an ocean, we're all sinking." This line from John Mark McMillan's song "O How He Loves Us" sums it up well. The truth is that God has given us a massive ocean full of His grace, love, and gifts. It is our job to simply begin recognizing and receiving them.

So as I close this book, my challenge to each of us is to begin to notice the many graces God has poured out on our lives. Whether that means writing them out as a list (thank you, Ann Voskamp, for this powerful challenge to us that is changing so many lives), or mentally taking note, may it become a new habit that begins to truly transform our minds and our lives in the process.

May God richly bless you in your journey of motherhood, and may you live in the fullness of His grace and abundant gifts!

Recommended Reading

These books and ministries are some of my favorites, ones that have truly blessed and ministered to me along my journey.

One Thousand Gifts by Ann Voskamp

Shepherding a Child's Heart by Tedd Tripp

Instructing a Child's Heart by Tedd Tripp

Loving the Little Years by Rachel Jankovic

Delight-Full by Kate E. Collins

Desperate: Hope for the Mom Who Needs to Breathe by Sarah Mae & Sally Clarkson

Anything by Sally Clarkson, including *Educating the Wholehearted Child* (an excellent homeschooling resource)

Lord, Please Meet Me in the Laundry Room by Barbara Curtis

Above Rubies magazine and other publications by them (a ministry to encourage wives & mothers)

Victory Over the Darkness by Neil T. Anderson (a wonderful book on our identity in Christ that was particularly life changing for me)

Acknowledgments

As cliche as it may sound, I must first thank God for giving me the opportunity to write a book, a dream that was in my heart since I was a child. But more than that, I want to thank Him for being the best parent in the whole world, loving me so extravagantly, and giving me the privilege of being His daughter. I also want to thank Him for all He has taught me in motherhood, through both the good and the hard things, and His commitment to my growth and maturity. God, thank You for giving me so many gifts in life, the greatest of which is YOU!

Secondly, I want to thank my amazing husband who believes in me and without whom this book would not even exist. Your love, support, and administrative help has been so invaluable. Thank you for being an incredible husband to me and father to our children. You exhibit the Father heart of God to them so well, and I would not want to be a mom without you as the dad!

Next, I want to thank my own mother, who has been such an example of sacrificial love for her children. Mom, thank you for all you have given to Jared and I, and for your continual love and support. I love you and am so thankful you are my mom. You are a great gift to me!

Samuel, Hope, Jeremiah, Joanna, and Isaac, you are each my greatest gift in motherhood. I am so thankful for the amazing treasures you each are. You mean the world to me, and I could not be more blessed.

Melanie Sunukjian, thank you for being such an awesome editor, friend, and support. This book would not be nearly as good without you! Michelle Ryan, thank you for your editing eye and encouragement, and for being such an awesome example of a mom who walks with great grace. Michelle Ahlswede, thank you for all of your help with the photo shoot for the cover, a labor of love for sure!

Greg, thank you for being so gracious as a publisher, and knowing my life as a mom is a bit hectic! I appreciate all of your patience with me and working on my time table with all of the details!

Last but not least, thank you to all of my wonderful family members in Isla Vista Church, for teaching me so much about God's love and grace. I feel like I am the most blessed person alive, greatly in part to each of you and the blessings you all are to me!

For more encouragement and resources on your journey into God's grace in motherhood, go to:

mom
Grace
.org